The Way We Remember It

Growing Up in Ely in the 1940's and early 1950's

Ann Powell
Michael Rouse

The
Ely Society

Dedications

In memory of my father, Harry Harding 1914 – 1996.
AP

For the past generations, the present and, most importantly,
Ben, Lauren, Lee and Cassie - the future.
MHR

Acknowledgements

Our thanks to the Editor for allowing the editing and reproduction of Ann Powell's
'Riverside Report' from the 'Ely Standard';
also to the Ely Society and in particular Michael Young, Pamela Blakeman,
Margaret Haynes and Virginia Watkinson, for advice and constructive criticisms.
Special thanks to Christopher Jakes, Senior Librarian Local Studies and The
Cambridgeshire Collection, Cambridge Central Library for permission to use the pho-
tographs of Ely Market Place, Ely High Street and The Cutter during the 1947 Floods.
The advertisements used within the text are reproduced from the
'Guide to the City of Ely' published by the Ely Chamber of Trade in 1946 &1952
and a guide published c.1936/37

Published by the Ely Society
8 Nutholt Lane, Ely, Cambs. CB7 4PL

2002 © Ann Powell & Michael Rouse
ISBN 0 903 616 21 1

Contents

Introduction

Michael Rouse

For years I had written down other people's memories, trying to recapture a world that was rapidly slipping by. I researched old photographs and put names to faces and dated buildings. In the early 1990's I began work on a labour of love, the story of Ely's cinemas for the Ely Society ('Talking Pictures', 1992). Again I interviewed people connected with Ely's earliest cinemas, I was on familiar territory. But then, of course, the story moved into the period of my own childhood and youth, the time within my own memory. It was strange to realise that I was, or my memories were, part of Ely's story.

I wrote briefly of what I remembered. I had always said that I had terrible recall of what had happened to me. That was true to a point, but as I grew older something strange happened and the past became clearer. The memories returned in short fragments, then longer anecdotes. My older son Ben who had just been born when I finished 'Talking Pictures', began to ask me questions about my childhood. So I began to write some of my memories down, as a record for my children should they ever be interested.

Around that time I was delighted to see 'Riverside Report' appear in the 'Ely Standard'. I had never known a time when the 'Ely Standard' hadn't been part of my family's reading. I remember my mother avidly reading the 'Social and Personal' and I always wanted to see what was coming to the cinemas. I enjoyed Ann's articles from the outset and was fascinated to see if she 'strayed' into ' my territory', but she rarely did. So I kept on working on my odd memories.

When I knew that the Ely Society was thinking of publishing Ann's pieces as a book, I volunteered to edit them, if I could add in my own pieces. I thought because we were only a year or so apart, but came from different areas of the town and had different experiences, that the two stories might work well together. That I will leave for you to judge.

I've enjoyed editing Ann's pieces and I think she has enjoyed reading mine. 'We'll have some fun with this, Michael,' she has said to me. And who am I to disagree with my Sunday school teacher?

I hope you have fun with these memories too and that they recall an Ely that you remember, or a time that you have forgotten, or an Ely that you wish you had known. There was a population in the Ely Urban District, as it was then, some thirty years before the emergence of East Cambridgeshire District Council, of a little over 8,000 people. There were gas lamps, dozens of small shops and pubs, no traffic or parking problems, hardly any tourism (unless you counted the evacuees and the prisoners of war)...but let us tell you about it, as we remember it.

The first voice you hear will be Ann's.

The Familiar Places

My grandfather was William Harding. He was born at Godmanchester in 1870 and worked as a Railway fireman. My grandmother had been Eva Cross from Burwell. From 1916 they lived in Ely.

My father Harry Harding was a driver for Drakes Haulage of Ely and for Esso. My mother Emily was formerly a Bidwell from Little Downham.

Her father was William Bidwell of Firth Head Drove, Little Downham. He was also born in 1870 and married Martha Jarman from Welches Dam.

Grandfather was a farm worker. He worked on the steam engines for threshing machines and ploughs. He also worked at the brewery in Ely, walking in from Little Downham.

When I was born in 1937 mother and father were living in Potters Lane, Ely.

Potter's Lane was not a healthy spot. I was born there behind the gas works, at No 4, one of five cottages on the right.

Next door, Marina died of meningitis at two and a half years old. Her father died a few months later of galloping consumption, his hacking cough could be heard through the walls.

Two public houses graced the Broad Street end of the lane. On the right was the *Royal Oak* and on the left, the *Black Swan*. Behind the *Black Swan* was the Gas Works Manager's house and Gas Lane. Benton's Farm House came after an area enclosing the Gasometers, then a little row of cottages with sunken floors stood at the gate of Barton Fields.

In the first of the Edwardian houses on the right after our cottages, Miss Smith gave piano lessons to a constant stream of budding musicians. The lane petered out into the first rough pasture field, the path leads on to the King's School Campus.

We played down in the dyke there, in the gnarled roots of ancient trees, where one of the springs trickles down the hill. We caught sticklebacks and took frog spawn home in the jar. Across the stream Martin's cows grazed the pasture, now the golf course. We played in all these fields. Only the Prisoner of War camp at the very top to the left of 'the hills and valleys' field was forbidden. There was a particularly interesting stream on the camp perimeter and a few old willows are still there.

I shall never get over the feeling that my territory has been invaded. The golf course covers part of my childhood and now the King's School has devoured the rest. The caterpillar tracked vehicle scraping the ancient grass away from the hills and valleys was like something from an American film about the Recession in the 1930's.

Another favourite spot where we went for a picnic was along Angel Drove, when it really was a drove and meandered beside the Campus. It turned up through a row of elms towards Barton Fields. Here on the dry drove a small camp fire boiled a kettle for tea and it was a great adventure.

It was also somewhat spiced by an old story that many years before an old lady traveller had built herself a bender in the ditch to end her days.

She died and sadly her brave dog guarded her so well, it had to be destroyed before anyone could approach. Children love being scared by creepy stories and that one has always remained in my mind. Whenever I go over Barton, I remember that faithful dog.

1937, Ann starting early at Ely swimming pool

My great grandfather on the Rouse side was William Charles Rouse who arrived in Soham sometime in the 1840's from his family home in the Benhall, Great Glemham area of Suffolk near Saxmundham. He appears to have cut himself off from the rest of his family and established himself in Soham as a blacksmith and vet. He married Eliza Bullman and they had fourteen children. Of them, Henry, my grandfather, who was a member of the Worshipful Company of Farriers, and at one time Parish Constable of Soham, took over the blacksmithing business in the High Street, and another son, Albert, became a vet.

Henry Rouse had eight children: William, Alec, eventually to move to Stanford-le-Hope in Essex and raise his family, Bert and Clem, both killed in the First World War, Edward, Ernest, my father, Reginald and Eva. William served as a farrier in the War and like his brother Alec returned safely. William with Edward went into the family business as farriers and general blacksmiths.

My father, who was born in 1903, left school at 12 and found what work he could – on the land, in a solicitor's office, a clerk at the Beet Sugar factory, and a Debt Collector and eventually as an Insurance Agent. In 1936 he married my mother Joan Onion of Ely.

The Onions, Onyons and later around 1940, the Unwins had been in business on Common Road (Prickwillow Road), Ely, in the early nineteenth century, probably first as market gardeners. John Henry Onion built a house next to his business as an agricultural woodworker in 1880. It was this house in which my mother was born in 1912 as the oldest child of Henry William Onion and Ada Maude Onion, nee Roythorne.

My grandfather, who had taken over the family business in his twenties when his father died, had four children, my mother, my uncle Douglas, my aunt Hilda, known to the family as 'Pip', and my uncle John. In the early 1930's my grandfather bought the land opposite his works and existing house and built a new family home, 'Roswell'.

My mother and father, with the help of a dear aunt, managed to buy their own semi-detached house in a new development off the Lynn Road in Ely in 1936 when they married. I was their first child.

I was born at 5 Lynton Drive in 1940. It was a small cul-de-sac almost on the edge of Ely just north of the 'Rifleman's Arms' public house. There was the Oakery just to the north of it then open fields, and a farm, a laundry, the ribbon of Orchard Estate, before the newly built RAF Hospital.

Dr Kenneth Maurice-Smith was the family doctor and he attended the birth with the midwife. My mother's sister, who was in the Red Cross, was also there, but my father was thrown out of the house in no uncertain manner and sought comfort in a neighbour's house until after I had arrived.

Lynton Drive was a new community. There were the Edwards', the Dunnells, ourselves, the Wrights, the Needhams, the Lanes, the McCallums, the Foulgers among the first 'settlers' on our side of the road and the Abbeys, the Newsteads, the Prices, the Speeds and the Carvers on the other side. The straight road petered out into an allotment area, useful in a time of 'Dig for Victory', not as if the houses themselves didn't have long back gardens. They did and on our side of the road they ran down to a small ditch that separated our gardens from New Barns Avenue and the houses and equally long gardens there.

On moving in, some of the men in Lynton Drive decided that they would buy a communal extending ladder. It would be kept in the Lanes' garage and borrowed by the 'shareholders' when they needed it for decorating or repairs. (It was still in the same garage sixty years later.)

We weren't, however, destined to stay there long. War having been declared, the decision had already been taken, especially as my father was waiting to go into the RAF, that we would move to my mother's family house, 'Roswell' on Prickwillow Road. And that would include Kay, our evacuee in her twenties, from London.

In the Black Swan in the days before the Welfare State, my dad paid his club money. Sixpence (2.5p) a week to generate a few shillings if the wage earner fell sick. It was common practice to pay in for a friend as well. He in turn paid in for you in another pub. I presume this was because only one amount could be drawn by an individual from each club. The amount paid out was about 3/6d (17p) a week. Each club had to close at Christmas and the remaining monies shared out among the members, which was a welcome bonus when budgets were tight. The evening started with free beer and sandwiches provided by the landlord. Later there was a kitty to keep the beer flowing and there were always homes where more of the club money was spent in the pub than went home.

Dad's boast was that he never drew a penny, but he enjoyed good health, many did not. Poor living, the effects of the Depression and bad working conditions, made sick clubs an essential part of life. Though there were always one or two who made sure they 'went sick' and had their money's worth, most were too afraid of losing their jobs to play that game. The man who died of tuberculosis dragged himself to work until he was too weak to turn the steering wheel of his lorry.

My earliest memories are therefore not of Lynton Drive but of 'Roswell', that big, square detached house standing on the slight bend in Prickwillow Road. To me, as a child, it had been there forever. In fact my grandad had had it built in about 1932. What gave perhaps the impression of greater age was that it had been built on a field that had a number of farm-yard buildings already on it.

The house was bustling with people and life. There was grandad Unwin, who had his agricultural wood-working business directly opposite, next to the original family home built by his father in 1880. There was grandma always off to the shops and quietly bustling around finding huge meals for everyone. And there were many mouths to feed. There was my mother, my father, my two uncles, my aunt, one or two evacuees. The war, of course, meant many comings and goings, but my early years centred around my mother, my grandma and grandad and that large house and its amazing gardens, orchards and field, down which my mother kept several chicken runs, so we were never short of eggs.

Grandad Unwin, Grandma in the deck chair, Auntie Hilda sitting on the grass, with Mum standing behind me, on the tennis court at 'Roswell' in the summer of 1942.

So we moved to Broad Street, a health resort by comparison, even if we did have a slaughter-house at the bottom of the garden. We moved, on a cold and frosty day, to No. 116, next to Newson's, the Butchers. Mr Newson would stand there resplendent in his white coat overall and striped apron sharpening his knives on a steel before he tackled the vast haunches of beef.

The crockery was packed into the little tin bath. Mum held one handle, dad the other and I held on tight to the side. There may even have been snow on the ground. We crossed the road from Potter's Lane to Broad Street. The bath started to swing, I slipped and shot under the bath into a heap on the road, being ticked off in no uncertain manner.

There was Haylock's corner shop, at the junction of Broad Street and Back Hill, presided over by Miss Baker. She was a large lady, given to wearing large dresses in plain or spotted navy, with lace edged modesty handkerchiefs pinned by little gold safety pins across her cleavage. She had corkscrew curls and bright red rose bud lips. One window of the shop was in Back Hill, the other in Broad Street. Imitation grass lined the window display of whatever vegetables and fruit were in season. Sacks of potatoes were stored underneath. On the shelves were a few tins and things, whatever was available in those wartime days. A few sweets, cigarettes, matches, odds and ends. No chocolate, no ice creams, not that I could remember chocolate and ice cream anyway.

Then we came to Graven's car showroom. Only one car, not for sale, no petrol, there was a war on.

Opposite the show room was St Peter's Church. My auntie took me there on summer evenings to sit beneath the six winged seraphim and listen to Evensong. It had a thriving congregation of maiden ladies, a choir of local boys, a Sunday School ruled by Miss Langhorn and an endless supply of budding priests from the Theological College at the top of Back Hill,

Next to St Peter's was Graven's proper business dealing with tractors, farm machinery and originally steam engines, which they shipped out to India and other exotic places. Young Ely soldiers in the North African desert came across an engine with 'J.Graven and Son' on the nameplate.

The Co-op occupied the rest of the building on that side to the corner of Victoria Street. A small door on the right led to the bakery. Here they unloaded sacks of Canadian flour, which had survived the wolf packs of the German Reich in the submarine infested North Atlantic. With them came a bonus. The sacks were not made of hessian, but of fine strong cotton and, joy upon joy, covered in red or green spots. These were soon washed and made into smocked dresses for small girls along the street. Before the shop proper there was a deepset door with a black and red tiled hall and steep steps leading to the shop flat.

As staff came and went so did a supply of fresh playmates. One had a very obliging old dog, which sat upright in my dolls' pram dressed in bonnet and dolls clothes.

The shop had two large windows and by then was only a grocery store. A short, dapper manager ruled the mixed staff of 'counter jumpers', as my father called them. He had been an errand boy at the International and knew all about 'counter jumpers' and often joked about ending up as an errand boy with a lorry. In the centre of the Co-op Miss Bidwell, like a Valkyrie with her blonde plaits round her head, held sway in the cash desk as the tubes of money whizzed in and out on the wires festooning the ceiling.

Jubilee Terrace, which commemorated George V's Jubilee in 1935, remained until recently a rough puddle strewn lane – the Cutter garden ran all the way down from the Tap, with a long wall topped with Birmingham Blues. The Martin children could climb over that. I couldn't.

It was always said that grandad wanted 'a big square house, full of six inch nails', and that was what Ambrose, the local builder, built for him. 'Roswell' stood level with Prickwillow Road, but on the Common side of it the land began to slope away. There was a wall with an advertising hoarding stretching along it. Behind the wall at the bottom of a winding path was a row of old sheds and stables. There was also a large open shed where wood was stored and my father's car because he was away.

At the back of the house there was a lawn with a path opposite the back door. The lawn was not very wide, planted with trees for each of his four children and then the path took giant steps down to the level of the field. Before the field, however, was the closely mown grass tennis court and shed. Two large Cox's apple trees stood at the bottom of the slope and the apples off the higher branches of one of them could be easily reached from the top of the steps.

Going off from the side of the lawn nearest Mr Broker's house next door was a narrow path through bushes and trees that ran along that boundary of the property to about the end of the tennis court. It was like a small mountain ridge it seemed high up above the court and on the

other side the land sloped away steeply to the gardens on Springhead Lane. At some time grandad or my uncles had built a wooden jetty on the slope looking out over the court. It was quite rotten and unsafe when I was a child.

It was a wonderful exploration when I was little, taking that upper path and braving the steep slope down to the tennis court.

In the field beyond the court were pens of my mother's chickens and various trees, including some very good plum trees.

At the bottom of the field was a fence and beyond that the fields fell away to the railway line and

Grandad's 'big square house full of six inch nails', from the lower level of the tennis court

the river. It is said that the dramatic contours of the field were due to excavating material for the railway embankment in the 1840's. I used to love to hear the trains clinking and clattering at night-time as I lay in bed. I could imagine the driver and fireman in the glowing cab as they puffed past the still dark pits, beside the silver river and rumbled over the bridges.

In the big kitchen cupboard were several sets of skates, fen runners. All the family told of how they would walk down over the fields in winter when everything was frozen solid to the flooded washlands there and skate for hours.

Next door to 116 we had a Bill Posting, with one large poster on the street and small ones on the side into the yard. These were usually auctions at the Cattle Market, the big ones said 'Guinness is Good For You' or 'Player's Please' or 'Dig for Victory'. Two cottages with dormer windows came next. In the first, the son of the family had such a horrendous speech impediment that the only way to understand him was to listen in paragraphs, but he was nowhere near as simple as strangers imagined. The other cottage was also intriguing. At one time it housed a young woman who was rather fond of the German prisoners of war. She nearly assisted one to be the 'Second one who got away'. They were picked up half way across the Channel in a rowing boat.

After four more cottages came one of those that stood sideways onto the street, there were several found in Broad Street. I remember it as a very poor home, bare brick floors and mats made of sacks. I played with someone there but can't remember who. A shop came next straight out of Dickens with bowed windows and a low ceiling. After the war it became a toy shop for a while.

Everywhere was crammed with people, evacuees, young newly married couples, servicemen's wives, nearly every home was shared.

A little further along the street the Miss Avelings kept the Post Office in a dormer cottage. Gas lit with a scrubbed brick floor, stamps and postal orders were dispensed through a small hatch in the wall.

Next door Mrs Collins ran a cigarettes and sweet -cum-fresh vegetables shop in what had been a fish and chip shop. The steel and tiled fish fryers were still behind the glass-fronted counter. Her speciality was brown pickle, which she sold in recycled jam jars covered with paper tops cut from the pages of an old Bible. She sold all sorts of things from glass prisms from Victorian lamps, that reflected the colours of the rainbow if you held them close to your eyes, to thick twigs of wood, which tasted of liquorice when chewed.

My grandad's workshop was a fascinating place. I watched him making long stacking ladders by hand. I saw the gates, the sheds, the cattle cribs, as they took shape amid the sawing, planing and hammering. I searched through the clean curled wood-shavings and sawdust for discarded 'Turf' cigarette packets. From them I collected the slides with their blue printed cigarette cards depicting famous footballers, cricketers or film stars. These were the last of the cigarette cards, which had been so popular before the war. Not that they were as beautifully printed. Real cigarette cards were sharp little pieces of card with lovely artwork and detailed information on the back usually published in sets of 25 or 50.

There were still plenty of them around when I was a child and we used to take bundles of them to school. There we swapped or played two playground games. One was 'dropsy', where the aim was to drop your card to cover another person's card, which you then won. The other game was 'flicksy', when you flicked your cards to see which card flew the furthest. It was not unknown for some enterprising competitors to stick two cards together in the hope that the added weight would give greater distance.

On one occasion, as I entered the classroom, the teacher suggested that I put my bundle of cards on her desk for 'safe-keeping'. It was, of course, probably to stop me fiddling with them. In the event when I went to reclaim them they had mysteriously vanished never to be seen again.

One marvellous day, when I was about ten my father arrived home with a small box. It had been given to him by Mrs Ankin, who had lost her son, Samuel, during the War. It was his collection of cigarette and other cards. She had kept them for him when he went away and now wondered whether I would like them. It was a treasure trove. I sorted them, looked at them, loved them and treasured them. How kind of her and I still have them.

Opposite was the woodyard, which scared the living daylights out of me when I had to fetch the wood as a Saturday chore. I was petrified of the crane swinging piles of planks across my path and the large round tanks, like ship's boilers where the wood was treated with creosote that took my breath away. Snell's shop, next door, smelled sweeter of old apples and cabbage stalks. Beside it there was a long yard down to orchards and the river.

A little cottage with a high-pitched roof came next, straight out of a fairy tale it looked. It was the oldest in Ely with low ceilings and higgledy piggledy rooms leaning on the Fish and Chip shop which then looked nearly as old.

Next there came the School House and the Girls' School, ruled by Miss Rickwood, she of the glass eye and the wicked temper.

Across the road, from the Park gates, the first shop was 'Ticker' Norman's which looks much the same today. A watch mender, he returned eventually from the horror of Singapore and its Japanese Prisoner of War camps to mend his watches again. A hat shop came next, then Denston's, another sweets and cigarettes shop, there were four sweet shops in Broad Street and no sweets. Very odd.

On the corner of Ship Lane stood Meadows' Gents Barbers. When I was small enough I went in the men's side to have my hair cut by old Mr Meadows, his moustache singed and turned ginger by an almost permanent cigarette. The men were not very keen on having children about the place and made pointed remarks. The salon was a treasure trove of stuffed fish and fishing trophies. Great pike caught and stuffed, swimming forever in their black-framed glass cases.

A public house called 'The Wheel' stood endways on to the path beyond Meadows' shop. It had, I think, an earth floor. Opposite a small shop, mostly empty, the man away at the war. But once, just once, they had some home made lead soldiers for sale. Someone had used the old moulds and melted metal. Unpainted they shone bright silver. They also cut tins in half inch curves down to the base, fanning them out and fixing bright blue and orange crepe paper flowers to each stem. Some sat in people's windows along the street, long after the flowers had faded to pale grey.

In the cottage next door was a basket maker and when the door was open to the passage the bundles of willows and finished baskets could be seen piled inside. Mrs Barker's shop came next, more sweets and groceries. She ran a milk round late in the day along the street. The milk girl struggling to balance a brass and silver coloured milk churn from the handle of her bicycle. Mrs Barker's temper was uncertain. It was brave child who went in there for sweets.

Right through the workshop was my grandad's garden with its promise of all kinds of fruit in season: gooseberries, red currants, black currants, apples, pears, plums, even walnuts, from a tree that overhung the garden from next door, and cobnuts.

My grandad was a very keen gardener. He must have been, for as well as the large garden at the rear of the workshop, he had another large plot on Cemetery Lane (Beech Lane) and an allotment just off the New Barns Road.

We were well supplied with fresh vegetables as soon as they came into season. Life, and the way we ate, was very much determined by the seasons. When there were plentiful runner beans, we ate plenty of runner beans. No one went hungry at 'Roswell'.

It was the same with the fruit. I loved the plum trees in the field, because they fruited early and the plums were delicious. Grandma would bottle them so they could be opened in the dark months when there were no fresh plums to pick and eat and grandad would store apples in trays in one of the many sheds.

My particular favourite fruits though were red currants, but more especially gooseberries, which grew on several bushes in the workshop garden. I would often nip down there. How difficult it was to wait for them to ripen. As soon as they were big enough, green and hard as bullets, my pockets were stuffed full.

Many a glorious stomachache was a small price to pay for an expedition there.

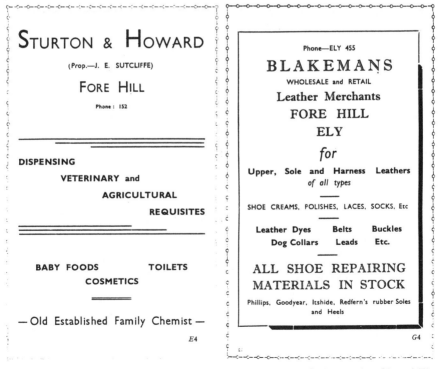

From the 1946 Guide to the City of Ely

From the 1946 Guide to the City of Ely

We Knew There Was a War On

We had a railway runabout ticket that last week before war was declared. Not that I can remember the holiday. I do, however, have a very clear picture of being crowded into a guard's van with piles of kit bags and soldiers in uniform.

I was jammed up against a set of pigeon holes in one corner which carried the internal railway post. Not that I knew that at the time. Many years later when I worked on the railway and I had to hand over post to the guard in its distinctive black striped yellow envelopes, I suddenly knew I had seen it all before.

So that was the last visit to the seaside before the beaches were covered in rolls of barbed wire and tank traps, until the year after the war when we went to Clacton.

That was an adventure. Our visit coincided with a very high tide. Camped out on the sand we knew something was up when the deck chair attendant came along the strip of sand slinging the empty chairs up on the promenade. We were not quick enough and the next wave engulfed us. Deck chairs floated out to sea, toddlers were held above our heads and we were very wet. I don't think I knew there were such things as tides.

I had never seen pineapples until then. A barrow on the promenade was piled high with them and one purchased for a treat. Big disappointment, too sharp, we all preferred tinned ones in syrup!

A correspondent to the 'Ely Standard', picking up on something I had written, remembered when he worked for the Martins at Barton Farm witnessing a young pilot fall to his death after baling out of an aircraft too low for his parachute to open. When I mentioned this two readers almost immediately were able to give me the sad details. The pilot was Jan Chalupa, a Czechoslovakian who had escaped from Czechoslovakia and made his way through France to England. He had joined the 310 Czech Squadron at Duxford. He crashed on October 16th 1940 during a routine training flight. I understand he was knocked unconscious as he baled out and in those days you had to pull your own ripcord. Some Needham's boys were in the field at the time with their schoolmaster and saw the aircraft in flames. One boy remembers fishing small pieces of the Hurricane aircraft out of the river where it crashed. Jan Chalupa was buried at Brookwood cemetery.

My correspondent also mentioned another incident when an aircraft crashed into the river bank near the Old Bathing Place.

I certainly remember the dent in the bank but I also recall the fuselage of an aircraft in the dyke on the right of the High Bridge. We played in there for ages before they took it away. Was it the one that hit the river bank?

I remember waving goodbye to Uncle Arnold at the gate in Broad Street. He went along the street, knocked at Ernie Ford's two doors down, turned and waved, and they marched off together towards the station. He used to tease me unmercifully as a child. He was just 21 when he died in the mud and slime beside that dreadful Burma railway.

Like many a young man in the Thirties, before the advent of paid holidays, he had joined the Territorials to enjoy the welcome break from daily routine. They were the first to march away and travel by troop ship, zig-zagging across the Atlantic, then back to South Africa and India, before arriving in Singapore days before it was over run.

An old photograph, self consciously posed somewhere in India, Sola Topee balanced on his knee and a cap badge with a scrap of red felt, are all that is left. But I shall always remember him as the laughing young man who told me he could make smoke come out of his ears

Uncle John joined the Home Guard at the start of the War. He was sixteen and wanted to 'do his bit'. Eventually he was a Private in the Beds and Herts Regiment and I remember just, I would have been three, this figure coming into the living room and putting a kit bag and rifle

down inside the door.

The next image I have is of me starting to come down the long staircase at Roswell and my father saying, 'Go back upstairs and stay in your room, grandma's had some bad news.' I saw grandma cross from the living room to the kitchen. I went back upstairs. It was late September in 1944.

At some time I would have been told, Uncle John would not be coming home again. He was in Northern Italy. His patrol, led by a young officer was attacking a house called 'Valergna' when they were surprised by a German machine gun. The details, as his commanding officer said, when writing to grandma and grandad, were not clear as the officer and all twelve men in the patrol had been killed. 'It was one of those unfortunate incidents which go to make up a war but mean so terribly much to the individuals concerned and especially their friends and relatives.'

I still have the last letter my uncle wrote to my mother He wrote it on the 19th of September in reply to her letter. He was killed on the 28th of September, so the letter could only have just reached us before the telegram bringing the news of his death. In it he says how we would all go to Hunstanton after the war and he would, 'take the old boy for a ride on the dodgems, I should think he would like that...we have got to make up for a lot of lost time and apart from that I am only twenty one.' He signed off 'All the best Johnny' with a P.S 'A few for Michael' and there was a row of kisses along the bottom.

I am sure there was a good reason for changing Railway Terrace to Castlehythe, but it is not as if the archaeologists know where Stephen's castle really was. The medieval maps, as is the way with medieval maps, are a little vague. The castle seems to hover somewhere around the bend in the river, which would be a strategic spot for a castle.

The Second World War relics emphasise the importance of this river crossing. If you look beside the river path just before the High Bridge you will see a concrete gun emplacement with a steel mounting for a Spigot Mortar. It had a man-size trench all around it. My cousin Ernie, as a member of the Home Guard, spent his twenty first birthday in that trench when the invasion was imminent.

On the other side of the High Bridge, going towards Stuntney at the end of the river flood bank, was a pillbox. This was a reinforced 'mini-castle'.

Between Ely and Adelaide along Whipper Smith's Bank across the fen towards Quanea is a similar pillbox out in the fields. But I digress, and so did the river. It changed course several times over the centuries, so pinpointing the castle would be difficult. I think it's under my garden. One day among the blue china chips, broken terracotta pots and misshapened flints, I shall find a coin or a scrap of armour. Well it makes gardening more interesting, if nothing else.

I was aware of uniforms, army khaki, the blue of dad's friends in the RAF enjoying some of grandma's hospitality and chasing me round the bushes in the garden. But I can't really say that I was aware of the War, as much as any child of that age is aware of what's happening in the world. I remember the importance of listening to the News on the radio and some of the newspapers and magazines with their stories of

Mum, with dad holding me. He was quite a stranger to me in these early years. On the back it says: 'At 'Roswell' , on leave from the Isle of Tiree, June 21st 1942'

the War. People might have come and gone, but being the only child I had lots of attention, or, just as happily, I was left to amuse myself in the vast space of the house and the gardens and workshops.

At the top of Castlehythe, where St Peter's Garage is now, there was a general haulage firm called Drakes. My father worked there as a lorry driver. He drove lorries about half the size of today's monsters. They carried local produce to Covent Garden, Spitalfields and the Borough markets in London. Return loads were picked up at the Docks – anything from flour to bird seed. A sadder return load was the worldly goods of evacuees as they fled the Blitz.

Locally they carted sugar beet to the factory at Queen Adelaide, and tanks of gas liquor from the Gas Works opposite, to spread on the land. Pre-war he seems to have carted the bricks for most of the local building when things picked up after the Depression. These included the yellow bricks for Barlow Terrace, opposite where I live in Annesdale, and the reddish mingles for Jubilee Terrace.

He draped the long rods of reinforced steel for the RAF Hospital over his little lorry and carefully drove them up Back Hill with them flapping and bouncing over the cab window.

The garage for the lorries was much the same corrugated building that can be seen today. There were, however, two cottages at the back, reached by the lane running at the back of Castelhythe. Lorry drivers lived in them. We lived close by in Potter's Lane, which was just as well because an early start was needed, perhaps two or three o'clock in the morning, to catch the early markets.

Wartime brought another dimension, prisoners of war. The lorries collected Italian POW's from the Cambridge Road camp and took them out to the farms to work. They were my father said, 'Like a wagon load of monkeys, full of mischief.' There was no antagonism. They loved children and patiently taught me to count – 'Uno, duo…' They made me a little willow basket with a double plaited handle and a silver ring from a florin, but that's another story.

I remember the harvest fields of my uncle's farm near Huntingdon in about 1945. The Italian PoWs were loading the sheaves of corn onto a cart to take back to the stack yard. Stocky sunburnt men from Southern Italy, they were proud of their strength and vied with each other to see how many sheaves they could lift on a pitchfork. One with the most splendid sun-blonded wavy hair caused a great deal of amusement among the English farm workers by insisting on wearing a hairnet.

Air raid sirens played a large role in my childhood. The alert still makes my heart stand still. We were bundled out into the shelter in the back garden and listened to the bombers grumble over.

They were not interested in us; the 'all clear' would sound and it was back to bed for a couple of hours. Then off would go 'Moaning Minnie' again and it was back out to the shelter. This was when we might cop a packet from bombs unloaded by the raiders on their way back from the industrial heartland.

Later the buzz bombs had us scurrying into the school shelters in daylight.

We had an air raid shelter constructed in the side of the slope from the lawn down to the tennis court. It was a home-made affair. I was taken there in one of the baby gas suits. Later we had a Morrison shelter serving also as a table in the living room. I graduated to a Mickey Mouse gas mask. It was red with round eyes and designed to be child friendly. But how anything smelling of rubber, that misted up so you couldn't see and felt clammy, could be child friendly, I don't know. However, it was good enough to wear and for me to jump out from behind a wall and frighten Auntie Pip.

Bearing mind there were no seaside holidays in the war years, the best holidays I ever had were, wait for it – at Mepal. My Great Aunt Lizzie lived at Low Bank, a real fen cottage long since replaced with a substantial house.

Low Bank had a thatched roof covered by corrugated iron. Rain water collected in a barrel from the roof for drinking. This was always boiled for tea or lemonade. You never ever drank water there.

Water for washing came from The Drain alongside the cottage, which was crossed by a very rickety plank. It led to a high bank with the Old Bedford River and the washes on the other side.

Uncle Alf, Aunt Lizzie's son, was an eel catcher and wild fowler. You can see him on the video in the museum with his flat cap on his head and old pipe clamped between his teeth. His punt guns hung on the wall.

Round a large table in the evenings we played cards – for money. Well, in truth, with the hoard of pennies and halfpennies kept in a large washstand water jug. They all had to go back.

There was a big garden and orchard behind the cottage. They were self-sufficient with pigs and bees. If a wandering swarm settled in the trees, we would all go outside banging saucepans and tin trays so they would drop into Uncle Alf's safe-keeping.

Once the pigs got out and I was confined to the house while everyone else chased around. Next thing I knew, a pig had his trotters up on the sill and his snout through the open window. I was petrified.

We must have had some sort of holiday at Hunstanton in 1944, as Uncle John mentioned it in his letter. I know we had a little caravan and kept it on Searle's field, near a ditch, adjoining the field where the donkeys that gave the rides were kept. I remember holidays there after the War, but I don't remember anything of that one in 1944. With the War situation easing, dad was able to get more leave and I suppose they were both anxious to feel that life could get back to normal again fairly quickly.

In the summer of 1945 we went to Great Yarmouth. I remember seeing the bomb damaged houses near the docks and being fascinated by the image of a building opened up showing the interior wallpaper, or doors on the second floor opening onto a chasm where the building once stood. This was what the War meant, I thought.

My grandmother must have been down there at the same time because she bought me a small tin drum in Woolworths and I recall walking across a little park with it. A toy drum was not the sort of thing to buy for a small boy really when you were staying in some small lodging house. I know ration books had to be handed over or some such arrangement, so I imagine the usual seaside treats were in short supply.

There was barbed wire closing off sections of the beach near the Brittania Pier, because of the mines that had been sown there.

There was a great deal of make do and mend from what I remember. A chipped tea pot spout was fixed with a separate rubber spout with a metal end, pots and pans, kettles and frying pans were soldered or holes plugged with metal washers. Split wooden handles were carefully and neatly bound with string.

There was no Sellotape or Evostick. Glue, which looked like toffee and smelled of fish bones and old horses hooves, was broken up with a hammer and melted down in a little double iron pot on the fire. Pong! It was terrible.

All crockery, glass and kitchen ware was at a premium by the time I was taking notice of such things. There were few replacements to be had during the war. The one or two thin Victorian or Edwardian water glasses my grandma had, alongside the chunky Thirties ones, worried me to death in case I bit a lump out of them. There was a little port glass too, with a broken stem set in a wooden cotton reel, that served as a medicine glass.

Oh dear, I've just remembered that awful red iron medicine that I had to take.

Dad was not often left in charge of me. In fact for the earlier part of the War, before my first birthday he was stationed away. I have cards written to me from him when he was on the Isle of Tiree in the Hebrides in 1942 and from Detling in Kent in 1943. It was only from about 1944 when he was stationed at RAF Duxford that he was able to get home more often. Well on one of these occasions, my mother took the opportunity to go into Ely for some shopping and my father decided to take me to a nearby field to pick some mushrooms.

We went past the end of grandad's wall, past the little cottage where the Convines lived, past 'The Dell', to a field at the top of the Common on Prickwillow Road, very near where Lisle Lane runs through now. There was a stream, sluggishly flowing through the field and cows. There were also mushrooms. But it was the cows that worried me. I was quite sure that their baleful eyes were fixed on me.

As father searched happily away for his breakfast, I watched the cows. As they stepped towards me, I stepped back. One more step towards me and I retreated again, this time falling backwards into the muddy, cowpat littered, stream.

My father lifted me dripping with water, mud and the unmentionable, and carried me at arms length back to 'Roswell'. I was standing in the bath upstairs still fully clothed having bowlfuls of water poured over me, when my mother arrived home. Poor dad, not even being a fearsome sergeant in the RAF police saved him from my mother's wrath and scorn. I can't remember whether we actually gathered any mushrooms.

During the war you had to register with one grocer and we were at the Home and Colonial in the High Street (where Barrie's is now).

It must be said we never went hungry during the last war and did not suffer from the bombing in Ely, but things were in short supply and some things a rare, if unknown treat. Occasionally a soldier or sailor would come home from foreign parts with bananas or oranges.

Come the happy day we were told to take a tin or jam jar to school to be filled with drinking chocolate from the Canadian Red Cross. None of the bitter old cocoa powder, this was sweet and smooth. Many fingers were licked and dipped into jars before we got home. I preferred it raw by the spoonful, it seemed a waste to mix it with water.

Then there were jumpers from the American Red Cross. There is a limit to how often you can unpick and reknit the wool you have. These splendid thick jerseys were super, speckled and tweedy. Had anyone ever seen double knit wool before this?

How did my grandmother manage? Every room of the house it seems, apart from the kitchen and living room was converted into a bedroom. The living room was packed full, as it contained a large dining table and chairs, grandad's roll top bureau in one corner, with the relay radio and candlestick telephone (Ely 142) on top of it, two armchairs either side of the large black range that occupied a substantial part of the side of the room with the airing cupboard next to it. But that is where we spent most of our time with grandma pottering back and forth from the kitchen opposite. She did have a daily maid, as many of the larger houses did. And she was a careful manager. I remember some years after the war seeing her break open a packet of loose tea and after she had tipped it into the caddy she carefully shook the leaves out from the folds of paper. When I questioned her about it, she said it was a habit that she had got into during the war years and had never stopped. She must have made up many cups of tea from the loose leaves. That was, of course, in the days before the universal tea bag. Tea or 'Camp' coffee were the usual day time drinks.

As I have said, she bottled fruit from the gardens and orchards. She pickled eggs from the hens down the field, and she wasted very little. What could be saved, paper, string, or whatever, was saved and re-used. The present age of packaging and buying unnecessary items, throwing away so much, would have bewildered her completely.

I have one of those memories that flickers away of my mother taking me to a room above the

'Club Hotel', overlooking the Market Place. It must have been the WRVS and they had a clothes exchange or second hand clothes shop. There my mother got me a 'new' pullover. There must have been many such similar economies and schemes in wartime.

When the war ended, food parcels began to arrive from relatives abroad. We had some in Salt Lake City, who sent I suppose tins of fruit and biscuits, but all I really remember were the sweets. Like big 'Smarties', layers of hard candy to be dissolved very slowly in the mouth. Delicious. And we made them last a very long time.

Lights played a big part in our lives. I was fascinated when the street lamps came on at the end of the war – albeit rather feeble gaslights – for I had been plodding about in the Blackout since I could remember.

We had gas lights at home with glass shades and mantles. Woe betide the person who broke the mantle by poking a match through the fine mesh. Out in the fen they went straight from oil lamps to electric lights, although a few had the hissing Tilley lamps for a while.

I had no idea what the popular song, 'I'm Going to Get Lit up when the Lights Go on in London' really meant, but I do remember seeing it on the Gaumont British news of Pathe Gazette at the cinema.

They floodlit the Cathedral with the searchlight battery from Witchford airfield and scorched a hole in the flag.

The men began to return. The year I was born Uncle Cliff was working flat out, sometimes all around the clock to complete work on the operating theatre for the RAF Hospital. At the end of that year having been called up into the Army he married Auntie Hilda, just before Christmas on his embarkation leave. He then left Liverpool with his regiment, the 1st Light Ack Ack, on the hazardous and awful three month sea voyage, zigzagging across the Atlantic dodging the U boats. Eventually they took on provisions at Freetown, then had a week's shore leave in Cape Town, before travelling up the east coast of Africa, through the Suez Canal to Port Said. From there it was to the deserts of North Africa and straight into action..

He was a gunner, with the first Desert Force, the 'Desert Rats', under General Wavell, then under General Auchinleck, when the force became the Eighth Army. Finally in August 1942 General Montgomery took command. He was there when the tide turned and when victory was assured.

Eventually Uncle Cliff left North Africa on VE Day and took the much shorter sea route through the Mediterranean arriving back in England ten days later. Soon he returned home to 'Roswell' and the wife he had not seen for over five years.

Uncle Doug had joined the Royal Engineers and sometime in 1946 he too returned home to give me lifts in the warm oil, petrol and creosote smelling cab of the little lorry, as he went out delivering ladders, gates and cribs to customers in the surrounding fen.

My father was more or less home by then, back and forwards to Duxford. Apart from Uncle John the family would be together again in 1946, in time for my sister, Elisabeth to be born.

Home and Hearth

Waking on cold winter mornings, I am truly grateful to hear the gentle purr of our central heating. It must be thirty years since I lit a coal fire and no amount of nostalgia makes me forget what a chore it was. Bearable perhaps, with a nice pile of old railway sleeper kindling and good bright coal, but what a struggle. Hot ashes that blew in your face in the lightest breeze, blacking the grate, scrubbing the hearth; then the wind would be in the wrong direction and it wouldn't draw.

What a game! And you had to make sure the chimney was swept regularly. I know a roaring fire is a joy to behold, but it was often too hot in front, too cold behind and how many young (and old) women toasting their shins regretted the scorch marks it produced.

Jack Frost no longer draws fascinating fern-like patterns on chilly bedroom window panes. No quick rush across cold lino to jump in bed and snuggle down into the feather mattress with a brick heated in the oven, wrapped in flannel or a stone hot water bottle to stub your toe on. A restless sleeper would kick them out with a crash waking the whole household. Feather mattresses were a bit like duvets, only you slept on top and wriggled down until the feathers cradled you like a nest. The feathers were all loose in the cover and had to be shaken back into place in the morning.

One thing I will concede. Toast tasted far better made on an open fire – provided you didn't drop it in the ashes, of course.

In those days housewives wore bright flowered wrap-around overalls with no sleeves, on top would go an apron to keep that one clean. When it came to a really dirty job to do, like scrubbing the step, there was a sacking apron with a bib that went over everything else.

Some time after the War had ended we returned to 5 Lynton Drive. My parents had let the house out to RAF personnel connected with the Hospital.

*It smelled strange and different. It was smaller than Roswell. A typical 1930's semi detached with two main rooms downstairs: the living and dining room and a front room for best occasions. In the front room was mum's piano and on it poor Mr Wills, the assistant organist at Ely Cathedral, later to be Dr Wills, **the** organist, struggled to teach me to play, stamping the floor with his foot as if to pound me into rhythmic submission. We lived, of course, in that back room with its French windows. We had a telephone (Ely 361), which stood on the window ledge of those French windows. Very few of our neighbours had a telephone and our number was willingly given to relations and friends to contact us if there was urgent news. In that way we became one of the first families in the Drive to share someone else's joy or sadness. But that was what being a 'neighbour' meant.*

There was a small kitchen, a smaller pantry near the front door, which was the furthest point from the kitchen. Upstairs two double bedrooms, a small bedroom and the bathroom.

The floors were relatively bare, stained wood with carpets in the middle, no fitted carpets. Upstairs there was lino with some rugs. The only source of heat was the coal fire in the lounge. It was so cold in winter that the ice formed on the inside of the bedroom windows and to put your foot down on the lino in the morning was to suck the breath from your body.

'A typical 1930's semi-detached' home

The houses had front gardens and very long back gardens, ours was partly laid to lawn, then a trellis and the vegetable garden with three plum trees at the bottom. Unusual plum trees they were too for the fruit was yellow and in a good season beautiful crisp sweet plums. We had an asbestos garage too as my father had a small Morris Minor car that had been stored in one of grandad's sheds during the war.

My Saturday morning chores in the 1940's consisted of queuing for sausages and coke, and I hated queuing especially in the winter. With meat strictly rationed, sausages 'off ration' attracted long queues. I had to be up at Holland's in Market Street (now Rayment's) soon after 8a.m. to arrive before the buses came in from the villages.

I used to hope that there would be no queue and a notice saying 'Sorry no meat'. Not that it happened very often. Usually when I arrived a few hardy souls already stood at the shop door and I faced a wait of nearly an hour.

Back down to Broad Street and collect the barrow to join the straggling queue for coke at the Gas Works in Station Road. Coke was a supplement to the fuel ration. What a rag, tag and bob-tail crew we were with old pram wheels, bikes and homemade barrows.

Muffled up to the eyes, scarves wrapped round and tied behind, but with bare knees, no long trousers or knee warmers in those days. Can you remember chapped legs and chilblains? Very painful.

I had to stand on tiptoe to reach up to the Gas Office window, handing over half a crown (twelve and a half pence) for a ticket. Retrieving the barrow and trying to avoid the weigh-bridge set in the road, which moved with the slightest weight, I trundled over to the scales. Here a begrimed gas worker loaded two large forks full of coke into the scoop and dumped it in the barrow usually tipping it up so I had to struggle.

Everyone was covered in dust, we must have looked like refugees anywhere in Europe at the time, but at least I didn't have to push my load up the hill.

We were a small community and we tended to stick to our own neighbourhoods. Ely itself though, was also a small community. When Dad came out of the RAF in 1948 he resumed his occupation as an Insurance Agent. He had his contacts through his insurance round. We tended to use the same tradesmen and shop in the same shops. No one, with the best will in the world, would have claimed that my father was much of a handyman. Certainly my mother had little faith in his skills and would regale us with stories of how Dad failed to tie the pram properly on to the back of the car and en route for Soham, as they drove up Stuntney Hill, they looked round to see the pram freewheeling back in the direction of Ely. (It was empty, of course).

So when a job needed doing he contacted the usual tradesman. Mr Harnwell was our regular painter and decorator. Bob Holland did all our electrical work. Mr Don Sindall, from Ship Lane, did any building work for us. When it came to plumbing then Dad always sent for Arthur Dockerill. As he huffed and puffed and poked around under our sink, Dad would nudge and wink at me, because in my father's eyes and mine, he was a hero. Arthur Dockerill had been one of the commandos on the St Nazaire raid. One of the most daring exploits of the War had seen him imprisoned by the Germans, eventually to return to Ely to unblock our sink or attend to whatever problem we had.

All around me as a child were people who had 'done their bit' as my dad would put it. Two doors away lived Mr Needham, who had survived being taken prisoner of war by the Japanese at Singapore with the Cambridgeshire Regiment. In the Butter Market Mr Long stood outside his little fruit shop and did not suffer boys, or anyone, to mess around with his goods. He was a real hero with the parachute regiment, and had probably frightened the Germans as much as he frightened me as a boy.

Sometimes Dad would come home with a rabbit recently shot for the pot and a gift from one of his 'Rising Sun' domino playing friends or from one of the many houses in the outlying villages that he called on for their penny or tuppence a week insurance. I would then be sent across the Lynn Road to find 'Nibby' Lee. 'Nibby' and his friendly wife and family lived in converted railway carriages set in a small farmyard and orchard. He was hugely larger than life, 'Come you on in, my ole booty, what have you got there, a rabbit? Give it over here.' Within minutes it was skinned and ready for a stew. There was nothing in that line of work he couldn't do, or wouldn't do for you.

Life had a predictable routine. Whether she wanted to or not, nearly every day mother had to go shopping for the food for the day's meals. That is Tuesdays to Fridays and often on Saturday mornings, although dad usually brought the joint of meat home. The milk arrived in bottles on the doorstep and newspapers were delivered by Burrows, and at one time we had regular deliveries from the 'Corona' man with soft drinks.

On Saturday evenings dad would go round to the 'Rising Sun' for a drink and keep up the acquaintance of the regulars and neighbours we had at 'Roswell'. He was never late home and would bring in, as a treat for me, a bag of Smith's crisps, find the little twist of salt in the blue wrapper. Later this became fish and chips for all of us from Croot's or Oakman's as it probably was by then. It was an enjoyable Saturday evening ritual.

Roast Dinner on Sunday with fresh vegetables from the garden. Dad, like most of the men, grew many vegetables and kept us well supplied from the garden. At the end of the summer, of course, we all went off searching the hedges for blackberries for eating raw, bottling or for mum to put into one of her special puddings. And all for free, apart from the scratches! Happy memories of the smell of cooking from the small kitchen, dad down the garden and 'Forces Favourites' coming from the lounge radio. While the oven was on, mum would bake cakes and pastries for tea.

Lunchtime was accompanied by the 'Billy Cotton Bandshow' and one of the comedy programmes like 'Life with the Lyons' or 'Educating Archie'.

From time to time, as became necessary, mum would get out the comb and hair clippers and cut Dad's and my hair in the living room under the light. We never paid to go and have our hair cut at the barbers.

Monday, of course, was washday come rain or shine, the small kitchen would be heaving with washing. Mum had a small washing machine with a little mangle on the top. The lino floor would get slippy with soapy water. On wet days the washing would steam on the wooden horse in front of the fire, on blowy or sunny days it would stretch in a line down the long garden path. It was cold meat for dinner, perhaps with fried potatoes, or salad in summer, as Mum didn't really have time to cook. It was definitely a day to keep out of the way and during summer holidays I would be sent off with instructions to stay out and play as long as I could. She was always home when I got home though and the door was never locked. No one had anything worth stealing, so why bother to lock up?

There was a laundry just up the Lynn Road from us, the other side of Butts Farm, but we never used it. Many of the girls who worked there lived in New Barns Avenue. They would come swinging along, arm in arm, laughing and chattering along the Drive to take a short cut through the allotments at the top to the Avenue.

As the evenings draw in, it takes me back to winter tea times and Children's Hour on the radio with Larry the Lamb, Dennis the Dachshund, Uncle Mac and Auntie Vi. But it is difficult to reconcile kind Auntie Vi with the formidable Ena Sharples she portrayed on television in later years.

Then there was Henry Hall and his Orchestra signing off with *Here's to the Next Time*. A commanding voice stopped the mighty roar of London's traffic to bring listeners some of the interesting people who were *In Town Tonight*, a forerunner of modern chat shows. At the same time the creepy voice of Valentine Dyal, *The Man in Black* and Paul Temple's *Coronation Scot* theme music brought drama to our firesides.

The wireless – a misnomer if ever there was one – had such exotic stations as Hilversum and Luxemburg, silent behind enemy lines. Only the sinister Lord Haw Haw reached us from the continent.

In any case, the wireless relied on accumulators to provide power. A heavy glass battery filled with acid had to be recharged each week at the *Walbro*, which stood on Lynn Road opposite the *Lamb*. Lines of batteries stood just inside the window with numbered discs attached to the anode. Woe betide the child who left the radio switched on and ran down the battery before the end of the week.

What really fascinated me was Uncle Prichard's crystal set. He was a great one for gadgets and never threw away a thing. This was a mahogany box about a foot square. On top was a crystal in some kind of holder. A couple of inches away was a metal probe mounted on a swivel. A pair of headphones were plugged into the box and you had to poke around the crystal with the probe. Then bingo! Suddenly there was a voice crackling in your ear. It gave me far more pleasure than just switching the wireless on.

My father said he could remember the first time he heard a crystal set working, the owner put the headphones in a large pudding bowl, so several of them could listen at the same time.

I loved the radio – real radio that is, the Home Service or the Light programme. Grandad and Aunt Rosa both had relay radios. The signal was collected in a building at the rear of the Public Room on the edge of the Butter Market by a business run by Mr Tom Kempton. From there the programmes were sent by a line, like a telephone wire, into receivers. No accumulators or batteries to be charged!

I listened to 'Children's Hour' at tea time, Uncle Mac and Uncle David were kindly Uncles. Early memories are of Toy Town and Larry the Lamb, 'Oh, Mister Maaaayor, sir,' he would bleat. Later 'Norman and Henry Bones, the Boy Detectives', were particular favourites of mine. What a surprise later to find that one of the 'boys' was Patricia Hayes, the actress.

We had tea at tea time, our main meal was dinner at around one o'clock. Dad would be counting his money out from his leather bag and entering the money paid in by his clients into his book. He would take his detachable collar off with the tie and put it beside the wireless. If we had visitors he would put the collar and tie back on again. He sat in his chair by the wireless, pen gripped in his huge hand recording everything in his meticulously small handwriting

From 'Children's Hour' we listened to 'Dick Barton, Special Agent'. With his friends Jock and Snowy, Dick fought foreign agents and spies and fifteen minutes episodes at six forty five each weekday evening, with a cliff-hanger ending every time.

I would listen to some of dad's favourites like 'Much Binding in the Marsh'. Later still I adored Paul Temple in the serials written by Francis Durbridge. Even today I cannot hear Vivien Ellis' 'Coronation Scot', which was its theme tune, without thinking of it. I enjoyed plays and series. There was a very good school series by Warren Chetham Strode, the name of which I forget, and, of course, 'Journey Into Space'. The radio was a wonderful trigger for the imagination. I would join the nation hooked on 'The Goon Show' and discuss it next day at school and, we all listened to 'Hancock's Half Hour'. Then, of course, as a young teenager I discovered Radio Luxemburg and listened in bed on a tiny mains radio. It was constantly tingling, as if it was about to pass on a really big shock. Thankfully it never did, but I was wary of it.

On Luxemburg I listened at night to the charts and Horace Batchelor, Keynsham, that is K–E–Y–N–S–H–A–M, Bristol, who offered listeners a fortune on the football pools. Any song I really liked and I would be off to Harpers on Fore Hill or Miller's, who had taken over the old 'Walbro' shop, in Lynn Road, to buy the sheet music. The charts were based on sheet music sales. My mother played the piano very well and would often bring in popular songs for herself. I played the piano, not very well, despite all the efforts of poor Mr Wills, but I enjoyed trying to play the hits of the day and anything else that caught my eye in mum's piano stool.

The advent of television did not have quite the same impact. People were used to films at the cinema. But we crowded into a neighbour's to see the Coronation of 1953. I found the snowy pictures a bit disappointing. But by the end of the decade we all had a television and reception was much better. It was like going to the pictures every night, a real treat.

The day suddenly came, in about 1951, when dad arrived home with a television. It was a Pye, nine inch screen, very large cabinet. It was not new, things we had rarely were new. One of those who had insurance business with dad was Mr Alps who had the radio, television and bicycle shop next to the Majestic. It was from him that we acquired our first set, the first television in the Drive. The only house with a distinctive 'H' shaped aerial fixed to the chimney stack.

I thought it was amazing, however much it flickered and crackled when a car went past or a plane flew over. Unlike my sister, I was a bit old for 'Muffin the Mule', but everything was a novelty. There seemed to be quite a lot of boxing and speedway on when they did broadcast for an hour or two in the evening. It was then that dad invited some of the neighbours in after they had finished their gardening. They would perch on the edge of the seats staring at this little black and white picture flickering away in the corner of the room and be enthralled. I would creep down the stairs and peer through the banisters at them.

Grandma, grandad and members of the family came round to watch the Coronation and dad sweated that the television would behave. I can't remember being particularly engrossed by it, but I enjoyed the celebration tea in the Central Hall, and duly collected my copy of the book about the new Queen written by Richard Dimbleby.

We didn't realise in those early days what an effect the television would have on us all. At first it brought the neighbours round, eventually it would, close the cinemas and separate us all in our own houses.

Sunday afternoon tea was the treat of the week. Summer Sundays saw us cycling out to Aunt Lizzie's at Low Bank, Mepal, where the bees hummed in the orchard and there was home made damson jam to tempt the wasps. The milk jug had a cotton cap edged with beads to keep the flies off.

Or we went along the dog daisy lined road to Grandma Bidwell at Little Downham.

My favourite was tinned peaches with evaporated milk, which you were expected to eat with bread and butter. If you didn't eat the bread and butter, you couldn't have the peaches.

Cutting the bread and butter was an art in itself and rather alarming. The loaf would be clasped in one arm to the bosom, spread with butter and then with a very sharp bread knife a slice of bread as thin as lace would be carved towards the said bosom. Even now it sets my teeth on edge to think of the aunts performing this skilled task.

Auntie Edie at Soham had been cook in service. Her Yorkshire puddings climbed out of the oven all on their own. Once rationing was over she made sponge cakes and Victoria sandwiches which looked as though they had been inflated with a bicycle pump. A lucky child would be presented with a pink, white and chocolate layered birthday cake about seven inches high. I had never seen anything like it.

I can remember a visit to an auntie who lived with a strict mother-in-law. I spent the whole visit confined to a large Victorian button back chair. I was not allowed to move or climb down for the whole visit.

Things were a bit better at my grandparents, but there was a lot of sitting on the settee with a book while they had forty winks. Any movement was greeted with, 'Hold your noise.'

I was not allowed into the front room to play. Not that I minded. The room was chilly even with a fire in the tiny grate and the chairs were hard and cold to sit on. There was a water colour of the Cathedral in the snow on one wall and a print of Rock of Ages on the other. On the over mantle were Chinese vases.

The kitchen was more cosy, even if I did have to be quiet. A big clock on the wall ticked those slow minutes away. On one side a picture of the young Victoria standing at the foot of some stairs in a shawl being told by kneeling ministers she was Queen. On the other, a Pears Soap beauty paused in a leafy lane to pluck some berries.

I was allowed down the garden but only on the path. I raced up and down swinging an old tennis racket pretending I was at Wimbledon. No ball, because I might have knocked it on the garden and spoilt the vegetables.

My dad's family for the most part were at Soham. His father had died in 1937. We would visit Uncle Ted living alone in the old family cottage beside the forge in the High Street. With Uncle Willie he was still running the business and there was plenty of work. Going through into the yard there was the strong smell of burnt hooves or singed hair, whatever it was, that smell pervaded everything. The cottage was low and dark with a sombre grandfather clock ticking in one corner and the sepia ghosts of two dead uncles in military uniform looking down from the walls.

Uncle Willie and Aunt Eva lived at 'Thorn Villa' with their two daughters Susan and Judith, while Aunt Eva, my father's only sister and the youngest of the eight children, lived at 'Herbert Cottage' with quiet Uncle Chris and their children Daphne, John and later Patricia. Uncle Reg and Aunt Ruby lived in Mill Croft with their son Geoffrey, who was Elisabeth's age, and later Barbara. It was a round of Sunday teas and playing in the streets, on the Recreation Ground or over the Common.

Grandma Rouse died when I was five, but sadly I don't remember her. Great grandma Rouse was long dead. But my mother's grandma, Great grandma Roythorne still lived in Chapel Street. She and her late husband, who had been Superintendent of Police at Ely and Deputy Chief Constable, awarded the MBE for his services to policing the community, had been very instrumental in bring up my mother who virtually lived with them. I used to visit great grandma in her cold Victorian house, opposite the chapel, where I was fascinated by the servants' bells high on the wall and the front room never used. She was kind, but always terribly old to me and the house felt gloomy and heavy with the past.

Auntie Ada was one of my grandad's two older sisters. She had been a dressmaker and seamstress with her own business in Market Street, but when I remember her she lived in a tiny cottage endways on at the top of Prickwillow Road. Even this tiny rented cottage was shared. She had a small living room with a bedroom directly above it up the steep narrow stairs. Her small kitchen was through the other living room and there was an outside toilet round the back. There was no electricity, she went to bed by candle light.

She was small and neat, always dressed in black with her grey hair scraped back into a bun. Once she took me to see old Mrs Harvey, widow of the second generation to own Harvey's shop in the High Street. Aunt Ada knew the family well and had done a lot of work for them. We went into a room above what is now the Oxfam shop and I was received as if by royalty, Mrs Harvey was very grand and gracious.

Harvey's department store dominated the middle of the High Street from the 'Bell Hotel' to the corner of High Street Passage. Around Christmas time, I think it was, they had a special display in one of the smaller windows. A slot had been cut in the window frame and we were able to roll pennies down a long chute for a charity collection. When Harvey's sadly closed in 1953 mum bought enough towels and bed linen in the sale to last us for twenty years. My sister tells me that she still has some of the linen in use. As she says, 'Where else would you get bolster covers?' I think the only sign that Harvey's was once there is the first floor window still engraved with 'Millinery'.

Aunt Ada kept her independence to the end. She had become a roman catholic and took me to the church in Egremont Street, which was always heavy with incense. There we would light a candle each. She loved children and had baby sat my mother and after me my sister. My abiding memory is of Aunt Ada sitting in her chair in the corner of the room beating time on a tin, while I marched round the big table beating on another one with a wooden spoon.

Christmas

The Germans added to our enjoyment of Christmas later in the war. They dropped streamers of silver paper to jam the radar. It was highly prized to make paper chains and trimmings. I gathered a huge armful up in Bull Lane in the field where Bell Holt now stands and carried it home with great glee.

In the months before Christmas dads and uncles would be working away making toys for Christmas presents. There were all sorts of magazines devoted entirely to fretwork. Patterns would be sent for and pasted on two or three plywood. Holes would be drilled in strategic places then the tiny blade of the saw threaded through, secured and shapes neatly cut out.

There was a Noah's Ark and all the animals, two by two, for my sister. A dolls' house for me, long gone, but I still have some of the furniture.

There were far more elaborate things: cuckoo clocks, covers for the *Radio Times* and letter racks. Just occasionally they turn up among the collectables on antique stalls. Gifts were in short supply and often home-made or second hand. I had a pram, a fairy cycle and an old pedal car passed on from evacuees and I played with them for years.

I found four old teddy bears in the loft a few years ago. One was knitted by my grandmother for my children and two from the 1960's who obviously belong to that generation and Robert's venerable old chap, very posh, made of real fur and leather, from around 1945.

My poor old Ted, who I gave a haircut between the ears with my dad's safety razor, was inherited from an evacuee. Ted was last seen battered and bandaged with his arm in a sling on a stall at the Christmas Missionary Sale held in the Corn Exchange each year. A label said 'Find My Pain'. I was grown up by then, my toys passed on, but I do have some very dog-eared *Rupert* annuals I wouldn't part with for anything.

With Christmas came school plays. This fair, frail little thing was cast as a fairy. To my delight I was fitted out in a beautiful green dress with a satin top and sparkling net tutu, but they made me keep my liberty bodice on underneath because of the cold. I was so embarrassed.

By Junior School I had graduated to the second king, in my older cousin's blue crepe edge-to-edge summer coat with dolman sleeves. And I proudly warbled in a squeaky voice: 'Frankincense to offer have I.'

It took me years to work out what Frankincense was. Gold I could understand and Myrrh had something to do with being buried, but Frankincense? Funny how nobody thought to explain these things.

On the lid of the battered old Christmas card box, I keep my lists and labels in, there is a rhyme: 'Let's go home for Christmas where the lights are shining bright.'
Home for Christmas has a certain air about it, a hustle and a bustle, journeys, welcomes, anxious parents peering out, a flurry of snow, a hint of frost. The relief when everyone is safely gathered in.

Most people are where they choose to be, but there are always a few far from home. It's a long time ago now, but I remember going carol singing with the Church Youth Fellowship in Queen Adelaide.

We went all round the village. Then we made our way along to the sugar beet factory where the campaign was in full swing, belching smoke like Dante's inferno, twenty four hours a day.

Beside the huts, where the men who came over each year from Ireland stayed, we sang our carols. They opened the windows to listen and contributed to our collection tins. They were a long way from home.

Sometime in the early fifties, I can recall getting up at 6a.m. and scuttling through the pitch dark streets to ring St Mary's bells for the 7a.m. service. Halfway up Back Hill in a darkened bedroom a child was beating on a tin drum and calling out loud enough to wake the whole street. So much for 'Peace on Earth'.

In the days when cotton reels were made of wood, my dad used to make hootie-tooties for us. Black and white cotton reels were shaped inwards like a waist. He would saw them in half push a piece of doweling through the hole, leaving enough at the top to grip and a little at the bottom to carve to a point. Then we would draw and colour a simple pattern on the top flat surface of the cotton reel. A quick twiddle with the fingers and it produced a fascinating toy – a 'hootie-tootie', a miniature spinning top.

We had other handmade toys: there was a sausage dog with its body waggling along on four wheels; a monkey on a stick, strung between two posts, a squeeze would send him tumbling over.

An old gentleman two doors away, stone deaf from the guns of the First World War, fashioned and painted the most intriguing toys. I had one like a table tennis bat with three or four chickens pecking in a circle, operated by swinging a weight underneath gently to and fro.

The German and Italian prisoners of war made toys for the children as well. I had a lovely little basket with two interwoven handles made by an Italian.

I remember two toy shops when I was small: Bolton's, on the corner in Market Street with High Street Passage and Sykes, across the road near the 'White Hart'.

The only toys I had from Bolton's, which I bought for myself, were dolls' house furniture. A black marbled fireplace with shiny red coals on the hearth and a bureau desk. Both of them sit in front of me as I write.

I still have my Rupert and Tiger Tim annuals, very battered and well read. Dolls were few and far between. There was one called Raggedy Ann inherited from a cousin and one beautiful new one I called Marie, in an emerald green knitted dress with a pale green silk crochet bonnet.

Somewhere around eight or nine, toys for girls petered out. Boys had Meccano, model soldiers or train sets for a few more years. But it was not long before girls had things like slippers and that old favourite, a manicure set. Not forgetting bath cubes, in hard square packages, or bath salts, coloured crystals with a spot of scent added.

There were always books, and one year a fountain pen. Filling fountain pens with ink was a messy business.

Eventually the Christmas present to have was a Stratton powder compact, another thing you see in collectables. I think I gave mine away years ago.

Childhood Christmas meant colour, warmth, excitement in the midst of so much grey, cold, dullness of the years after the Second World War.

Those Christmases of my early years must have been strange with the men away and presents hard to come by. I still have the Active Service Edition of the Bible with the RAF badge stamped on the front that my father sent me for Christmas 1943:' To Michael, with much love from Daddie xxx, Detling 1943'. Detling was down in 'bomb alley' in Kent, and I suppose it was impossible for him to get me any other present.

It is Christmas at 'Roswell' that I always think of first. I have a letter written by my grandma to Uncle Doug while he was in the army. He would be spending Christmas In Scotland. It is undated but it would be 1945. "This is Sunday night and we are all here. Auntie (this was Aunt Ada, who spent every Sunday at 'Roswell' at this time) reading to Michael. Pop reading, Ernie (my father) writing and Pip (my aunt) dressmaking...Mrs Churchyard paid me for six boats on Saturday and the others I put in Comins Xmas toy sale, so you will have a little money when you come home."

I remember these little boats, carved out of wood that my uncle made. They were painted silver. He must have made a number of them to wile away the hours. There were several that stayed in the house.

Since my grandad and my uncle were carpenters sometimes I got brightly painted wooden toys that they had made. Uncle Doug, one wartime Christmas while he was still in the army travelled home for Christmas and brought me a wooden jeep he had made from odd bits of wood, wire and canvas. How I loved it! I also had a rocking train that I could sit on. That was made in the workshop and a real favourite toy. I must have been given that for Christmas 1945, for a letter written a few days after Christmas by my grandmother to Uncle Doug is about the Christmas presents. "Michael has been riding his engine to death, no doubt that's the best toy he has had". The same letter mentions a trip to ' The Bell' , which was the family's favourite place for a drink in the town. It was the epitome of the small market town hotel.: "Pop took me up to 'The Bell' on Thursday night for an hour, but there were no bright young things there so it was rather tame." ('The Bell' in the High Street, now Lloyds the Chemists, closed in 1959.)

Another year Uncle Cliff, home at last from the North African desert gave me a large wooden bomber that he had carved. By means of a piece of dowel in the top and a wooden bomb fitted snugly into a bomb bay, I was able to bomb my lead soldiers into submission. A few years later he gave me a little engine that worked on sharp-smelling methylated spirits and took some getting going.

Just before Christmas Miss Willink, who conducted the Sunday School would take a group of us, including several of my Silver Street school pals, to her little cottage. It was a short distance from the church on the edge of Palace Green. In it she had a trunk. In the trunk were clothes for dressing up. We would sort out the costumes for simple plays telling the Christmas story.

One year, I remember, we performed in the little St Peter's church where I had never been before and we even ventured as far as Prickwillow and put on the play in the church there. Whenever I hear some of those familiar Christmas words 'Therefore with angels and archangels and all the glory of heaven.' It is my own ten year-old voice ringing out and I think of those exciting moments in those dark Christmas churches.

When I was ten, I was chosen to read a lesson in a combined schools' service in the cathedral. With the octagon towering above, I stepped forward, all short hair and short trousers and read from St Matthew some of the most timeless words in the English language:

" Now when Jesus was born in Bethlehem of Judaea in the days of Herod the king, behold, there came wise men from the east to Jerusalem…"

The period before Christmas despite such activities was really an agony of waiting. Letters had been written and despatched to Father Christmas through the fireplace. Small gifts had been bought for others and the Christmas case had been brought out, placed on the peg rug in front of the fire and the paper saved from many previous Christmases had been picked over again and re-used. How I loved some of that paper with its familiar and magical designs.

Another case contained the decorations with chains that could be looped and festooned around the room. Grandma had some lovely tissue paper balls and bells that lay flat then opened out to be suspended about the room. Sometimes I would be organised to sit and make paper chains out of strips of coloured paper using flour and water paste to stick them together.

Most of the shops would have displays of their Christmas goods, but I don't remember many bright lights.

In the week before Christmas the Christmas issues of the children's comics would appear with snow-capped letters and holly decorations. Desperate Dan would have an amazing Christmas pudding capped with snow or perhaps it was custard, I could never tell. Snow-capped comics and Christmas cards landing on the mat meant that the day itself was creeping, oh so slowly, closer.

There were visits to be made to my great grandma who still bustled round her otherwise empty house in Chapel Street, full of the ghosts of the past; to Auntie Rosa on Cambridge Road, who sheltered the ancient and deaf Uncle Frank and his invalid sister Auntie Flo, who never seemed to leave her darkened room and to Aunt Ada, at the top of Prickwillow Road. There was a trip to Soham to visit more uncles and aunts and cousins and to the family forge where Uncle Ted lived alone cocooned by his deafness. ' Merry Christmas, Happy New Year'…then pleased to be home.

There were parties around Christmas time. When my father was still in the RAF police at Duxford, I went there for parties. I remember how I hoped that my present from Father Christmas' sack would be a clockwork toy car and how delighted I was when I got one. Later there would be British Legion Christmas parties in their hall just off the Range on Silver Street. After we had moved back to Lynton Drive on Christmas Eve we made the short journey across Ely to grandma and grandad's house for the family gathering. It was like going home.

The fire would be laid ready in the front room, where the Christmas tree stood sheltering the brightly wrapped parcels not to be opened until Christmas Day. We would all be in the back room and the kitchen. There would be one of grandma's special suppers and grandma, my mother and my aunt would work on the preparations for the next day's food. My father and my two uncles would cross the road to the 'Rising Sun' for a seasonal drink, thoughtfully getting out from under the feet of the busy women.

And I would wait in an agony of rising suspense for bedtime but knowing it would not bring sleep because I was too excited.

In bed, the room I shared with my mother and father was above the front room. On the mantelpiece immediately below me in that front room was a chiming clock. It chimed every quarter with a Westminster chime and then struck the hour. How I lay awake sensing the hands creeping round and then hearing the chime. I would hold my breath in the dark ready to count the hours..ding, dong, ding, dong; ding dong, ding, dong; ding, dong, ding, dong; ding, dong, ding, dong...**dong** . One o'clock? I couldn't believe it. It was always one o'clock and I was hoping it would be six o'clock when I might explore the pillowcase at the foot of my bed.

I would eventually fall asleep and when I awoke and felt with my feet and could make out the lumpy pillowcase and hear the soft rustling of the paper I knew that he had been. (Father Christmas was always **he**!)

My parents would contain me as long as possible but eventually I would be sitting up in bed delving into the white coldness of the pillow slip and pulling out the various lumps and bumps of the long-awaited surprises that Father Christmas had found for me. Outside the road was quiet and all was dark, but gradually the household awoke, someone would go downstairs and put the kettle on and various members of the family would look into the room on their way for a cup of tea.

Of course, the presents, when I was small, were small and simple things: a ball, magic colouring books, pencils, paints, a jigsaw puzzle, a kaleidoscope, a cap gun, toy soldiers, sweet-smelling plasticine in brightly coloured strips, marbles and Christmas annuals, 'Tip Top', perhaps, or 'Film Fun', 'Radio Fun', 'Beano' or 'Dandy', so many to enjoy. It was all magic whatever came out and got placed onto the bed. (Except, of course, the useful and essential items from Father Christmas like vests, underpants and socks, how thoughtful of him.)

There was one Christmas when my father went downstairs and as he was coming back up, I heard my uncle say 'Couldn't Father Christmas get that down the chimney?' and I knew it was the bicycle I wanted. In fact I could smell it before it got into the room. It was not new, such items rarely were, but it had been newly painted and done up, and it was the bike I had asked for and it really was just what I wanted.

My morning was spent reading, playing with my toys and keeping out of the way, while the cooking of the dinner went on. Often we would have a cockerel from the field or one of my grandad's many business contacts, one year it was a goose, which he had kept in the yard next to the house and fattened up himself. It was a nasty, aggressive bird. I hated it and was greatly relieved when its moment of glory came on our Christmas table and it could no longer terrorise the yard.

Christmas Day had a strict ritual. After dinner, the women washed up, grandad fell asleep in one chair, my uncle who lived there would begin to fall asleep in the other fireside chair, while my father and my other uncle would disappear to find the bowl of walnuts and cobnuts.

It was important that my uncle did not fall asleep because he had to go down the field and feed the chickens. This had to be done before the King's broadcast at three o'clock. By three o'clock all the clearing up would have been done and everyone gathered in the back room to listen to the solemn broadcast on the relay radio, which stood on top of grandad's roll top bureau.

The end of the broadcast meant that we then moved to the front parlour. The fire that had been laid waiting for days was now blazing and the room was warm; it was time for the tree and its presents.

Presents were handed round one at a time. Most of the adults seemed to know with nudges and winks what every parcel contained, except my grandad, who was always delightfully surprised by everything he was given and everything he gave.

There were presents for me from the family. Always there would be a' Rupert' annual and the idea would be to give it to me to keep me quiet while all the presents were being exchanged. Happy memories of the gifts piling up at everyone's chairs, grandma collecting the paper, so carefully removed without tearing and the string, for re-using next Christmas. (How she hated it when everyone began using sellotape and the paper tore.) The room would become hotter and hotter but I was off to Nutwood with Rupert Bear.

A favourite toy was a construction kit, a forerunner of Lego, but not as sophisticated. It was called 'Bayko' and involved putting small steel rods into a baseboard and sliding panels of bricks, doors and windows between them to make a house. There was a roof to place over the house. It wasn't very versatile but I played with it for many happy hours.

Later there would be games, quizzes and mother would go to the piano and father would stand alongside her and sing ' I'll Walk Beside You' and 'Bless this House'....

*And finally I would go sleepily to bed hugging my books and presents. Tomorrow would be Boxing Day, my grandad and uncle would be off to see Ely play football, I would have toys to play with, but after all those weeks of waiting Christmas was over for another year and more grey days lay ahead, but **He** had been, Father Christmas hadn't let me down. No one had - it was a lovely Christmas.*

When I was eleven I began helping with the services in the cathedral. I particularly enjoyed the Christmas Eve service where we processed around the cathedral. It began with the solo voice singing 'Once in Royal David's City', and a shiver ran though me then, as it still does today. I would carry a candle between the choristers; later I carried the cross at the head of the procession.

Then it was out into the cold night air under the massive shadow of the cathedral, reclaim my bicycle from the railings by St Cross Green, out into the gaslit streets and pedal happily home with the lamp flickering on the road ahead of me. There were a few people about and some Christmas trees winked from front parlours. There would be supper at 'Roswell' and the big day was even closer. I was as excited as ever.

From the 1946 Guide to the City of Ely

Childhood Haunts

One of the good things about spending part of your childhood living opposite a public house was the cheery sound of voices especially in the evenings as customers left. There was no slamming of car doors because everyone walked or cycled. In this period after the Second World War there were over forty pubs in Ely so there were enough for everyone to truly have a 'local'.

Our local was the 'Rising Sun' on Prickwillow Road, standing right next to my grandfather's workshop. It was one of those double-fronted buildings with a door in the middle. Customers were served in one of the front rooms while the rest of the house, apart from the small room where the beer and spirits were kept, was a family home. This was quite common with the smaller public houses. It had been built by Obed Cross in 1847 (see 'Ely Memories' published by the Ely Society, 1998.)

It was a real beer and dominoes pub with the men, I rarely recall seeing any women there, sitting around quietly supping their beer, shuffling their dominoes and talking.

The landlady was Mrs Polly Plumb, always welcoming, cheerful, chatty and especially kind to me, as were her husband Frank and her two daughters. As a child I often called round to see them and usually returned home with a copy of the 'Dandy' comic. In fact the 'Dandy' was still being sent on to me when I was nearly twenty.

When we returned to Lynton Drive, the 'Rifleman's Arms' was just around the corner and again often at night when I was in bed I could hear the cheerful sounds of the men coming out at closing time. I liked it, there were people around, it was comforting.

In the summer of 1994, they pulled down my small corner in Victoria Street. The primitive Methodist Chapel had been there for over a century, the Schoolroom and Manse were a little younger. As they pulled the Schoolroom apart, I was surprised to see the old wooden panelling still in place, having survived conversion to a factory office. It had been the back of the wooden bench running round the room where we sat and sang:

> "Jesus bid me shine,
> With a pure clear light.
> Like a little candle,
> Burning in the night.
> He looks down from heaven,
> To see us shine.
> You in your small corner
> And I in mine."

Here we were taught, long before we could read, the stories of Noah and the Ark, Moses and the bullrushes and Daniel in the lions' den. 'Dare to be a Daniel – dare to stand alone'. There was the fiery furnace with Shadrach, Mechack and Abednego. We heard how Jesus walked on water and turned water into wine. For Sunday School Anniversaries, we each memorised our poems and Bible readings. Sometimes we attended the adult services in the Chapel being allowed to leave before the sermon, thank goodness. A bigger boy, Gordon, was often called on to pump the organ. The Minister's prospective son-in-law, home from the war, in his smart RAF uniform, cap folded under his epaulette, played the organ for the services and we sang our hearts out:

'Shall We Gather at the River', 'Til we Meet at Jesus' Feet' and 'Onward Christian Soldiers'.

My days at Chapel were numbered, however, I really belonged to the Church of England and St Peter's Church in Broad Street. I was baptised there a few days after George VI was crowned in 1937. How I joined the Chapel I am not quite sure. I think they had a keen teacher who rounded up all the children. It served me well though, as much at home in Chapel as in Church. They have the best hymns, but the sermons are too long.

We played in the garden but also out in the street. The Drive was a cul-de-sac and there was hardly any traffic. I think only three families owned a car in the street, so we played street cricket up against the gas lamp standard and street football without many interruptions.

At the Lynn Road end was an area we called 'The Dump'. It was a largish plot with several massive oak trees, part of Canon James Bentham's planting of oaks in the 18th century and why The Oakery was called what it was. In fact just past The Oakery is an obelisk commemorating James Bentham's works.

Everyone cut a path across 'The Dump' and we climbed the trees there. Many of them had notches hacked out or large nails hammered into their lower trunks to help us get up into the branches. How I envied those brave ones, who would climb to the very top and stand like a 'button boy' with arms reaching up above the top of the tree. I was a poor climber soon finding I disliked heights. We built camps in the usually dry ditch down one side of it. It was like an adventure playground and every now and then we children would undertake a clearance of the nettles and put ashes on the path or general tidy 'The Dump' up.

At the other end of the Drive we steered clear of the allotments as many of them were being used. We walked between them to a field where we held the games of football and cricket. We wore a sizeable area quite bare of any grass and played on the dusty surface. Boys from New Barns Avenue would come over and there would be large and vigorous games until we were called in for bed.

Apart from the Chapel, the street has changed very little. The house and cottages have been modernised, but there are hardly any children now, which is perhaps a good thing, as speeding cars anxious to beat Broad Street's jams, would make short work of any child dashing out to play.

On the left, at the top of the street, where until recently cars swooped in to have their exhausts replaced, was the Co-op yard. I can vaguely remember horses in there. A large grocery shop fronted out on Broad Street with a bakery at the side. I delivered a daily paper to the Head Baker through the yard. Each morning he gave me a bag of yesterday's currant buns. Now there is a limit to how many stale buns you can eat. Most of them ended up in the chicken run or they made a scrumptious trifle on Sundays.

On Saturdays he gave me fresh jam doughnuts. It must be remembered that the Head Baker came from a generation of boys who often went hungry if they came from poor homes. By the time I was doing my paper round, although war time rationing was still in force, few went hungry. However, you did not turn your nose up at currant buns.

Just around the corner next to the 'Rifleman's Arms' was a little row of cottages, later cleared to make a car park. In one of them lived George Bell and his wife. They were always kind and welcoming when I wandered round there. Across the road and towards Ely was a small wooden shop owned by Mr Cross. Like Uncle Cliff he was home from the Eighth Army. It was a small general stores and we headed over there usually for sweets, especially when they came off ration and for ice creams. One hot summer we had a craze for apple ices. These were slabs of crushed fruit frozen and wrapped in foil. They were delicious, very sticky and messy, but we loved them. They were not only made from apple, there were plum ones and I think rhubarb ones, but we always called them 'apple ices'.

Victoria Square came next to the Co-op and Victoria Street. It was once called Miller's Square, presumably re-named in honour of Queen Victoria's Jubilee. A metal post in the entrance afforded continuous amusement to the children who dared to leap frog over it. I never dared, but the large robust family of Martin children hop, skipped and jumped over it all day.

The Square of nine or ten houses was full of children and old people. It teemed with life. One mother's voice was so strong we could hear her calling her children from our house in Broad Street. The biggest family lived in the smallest house, where did they all sleep? The eldest was about thirteen and there was one for each year down to the new baby.

Next to them was an old couple who kept a small holding down Stuntney Road. Every day they set off to work on the land on their bicycles, with the old dog riding in an oil cloth shopping bag hanging from the handle bar with just its head poking out.

My Auntie lived in one of the bigger houses, three bedrooms, front room, kitchen and scullery – and an inside lavatory - the only one I knew. Everyone else in Broad Street had outside lavatories, even the Landlord next door.

There was a drain in the middle of the square to be avoided on a bicycle. The boys played cricket, wickets chalked on the wall, or dug small holes in the dust for a game of marbles. Marbles were in short supply being wartime and what few we had were inherited from older children.

Mondays the Square was a 'no go' area. Washing lines stretched from corner to corner and woe betide the child who dared to cycle or run through the drying clothes in case they knocked a prop and let the washing down into the dirt.

Just after the First World War, a sailor son of the Square brought a monkey home. It settled down in his home, slept in the hearth, but sadly died of cold in winter. It was buried rolled in an old velour school hat in the gardens. I wonder what the archaeolgists who have been digging nearby recently would have made of that.

Cutter Lane ran down the side of the houses on the far side of the square. The *Cutter Tap* formed the other wall of the lane. I once remember fighting my way in through the black-out curtains over the door to the smoky rooms behind on an errand to fetch the butcher back to his shop for a dinnertime customer.

There were a number of us children up the street in those years after the war: Andrew Newstead lived nearly opposite. His father was a big, quiet man, who after a day in the family wet fish shop could often be seen steadily walking up the Drive in his wellington boots carrying his fork and spade, or hoe, heading for his allotment. John Wright, who lived next door was more my sister's age, Peter Speed, whose father like mine was an insurance agent, was quite close in age to me. There was James Coote from further up the Drive, Roger Lane, who was a bit older and there were Paul, Michael and Neil Homes from nearby on Lynn Road, Barry Staines, Michael Barker from just along Lynn Road. We played variously and then went our separate ways.

Now let me take you back to the cold wet spring of 1947. I am ten years-old and paddling in the flood water on Annesdale Quay. A large barn stands where the town houses now face the river. Annesdale House is three cottages. There is no riverside walk, the *Cutter* is flush with the water. A few steps lead down to the river but these are under deep flood water, which is creeping along Annesdale and up Victoria Street.

To stand by the High Bridge in the teeth of the wind, the water brimming over the banks in choppy waves, men dotted along the banks at intervals as far as the eye could see watching for the telltale spurt of water half way down as the relentless pounding scoured beneath the waterline, was something I shall never forget.

The swans came marching up into Broad Street and we fed them from the front room window.

There are small cottages and houses all the way along the east side of Annesdale. Castlehythe is called Railway Terrace. Nearly all the householders are railwaymen, gas or brewery workers. The gas works is on the other side of Station Road filling the air with fumes that gnaw at the stone crosses on St Peter's Church. Eventually one will fall away nearly crowning the priest in charge.

The water laps along the boathouse wall. I paddle along slowly, the water within an inch of my boot tops. One false step and they are full of water.

I am informed when I squelch home, that, had it not been my birthday, I would have had a good hiding.

These streets were my playground. On the quay in summer stand Appleyard's elegant rowing boats and varnished canoes. Once we could swim it was a few pennies to take a canoe out for an hour. That was long enough to paddle up to the Old Bathing Place, near Wells Engine, halfway between the High Bridge and Newmarket railway bridge. On the left, the White Bank and its shallow places to paddle, one a large dent made by a fighter plane which crashed there.

Between Appleyard's boathouse and the first rail bridge, there was another cut, where the Sea Cadets stored their boats. Their drill hall was at the top of Victoria Street.

Do you remember the swimming pool in Angel Drove? Ah! Happy days. The water was freezing at the beginning of the season in May. It was like jumping into splinters of ice. It took your breath away.

Ann at the Swimming pool, Angel Drove, 1952

What's the temperature? That was the most important thing to the anxious queue of youngsters waiting to gain entrance for four old pennies in the 1940's.

Over the door it said, 'EUDC 1933'. It was a 25m pool, well below ground level, with a concrete surround, grassed slopes and steps leading up to terraces and wooden cubicles, males on the left, females on the right.

Just inside the door a long open changing room with a canvas curtain gave a modicum of cover for those girls unlucky enough to find the cubicles all taken. Modesty was important in those days.

The wind caused a few shrieks when it flapped the canvas. The cubicles smelled of damp wood soaked in chlorine, warmed by the sun. The race was on to be first in the water. Of course, you could always have your costume on underneath if it was dry, but after a morning session there is nothing quite like pulling on a wet wool bathing suit in the afternoon. I mostly had the standard black wool costume. Hand-knitted ones sagged disastrously. A stretch one, made from bright yellow parachute material with shirring elastic, turned transparent when wet. A green rayon one was better. I can remember hanging on to the ends of the material as it fed through the sewing machine and the elastic gathered it up. Bikinis appeared on the scene, but they were not allowed in competitions in case you left the bottom half behind.

The pool had a slide, three diving boards and a spring board at the 8' 6" deep end. The shallow end was 2' 8". There was a thriving swimming club, which competed with other local clubs.

The temperature of the pool very seldom reached the 70F mark. One hot summer it crept up to the 80's, but the spectre of polio stalked the land and the pool was closed, leaving us high and dry. Some took to the river again where the earlier generation had learned to swim.

Mother had learnt to swim at the old swimming place in the river up near the Newmarket railway bridge. My early attempts to swim, I don't remember any lessons as such, were in that open air pool. I remember that mixture of smells of chlorine and gas from the gas works down there, but most of all the fact that it was so cold. I was one of those thin kids, 'I've seen more meat on a butcher's pencil', and I didn't enjoy swimming. My father had done a lot of swimming and won races at Soham. For years he was connected with Ely Swimming Club, but it wasn't for me.

Grandad Unwin, family told, was one of those swimmers who could swim steadily and forever, right out to sea at Hunstanton and then flip over onto his back and float. But he was a superb all round sportsman and as much as I tried. I couldn't emulate him.

He had been an outstanding footballer for Ely City and carried on a lifelong connection with the Club ending up as President and my Uncle Doug followed him. Football was the sport at 'Roswell', and tennis, but mainly football. I followed the fortunes of Ely City Football Club and as a youngster went to as many matches as I could. We stood two or three deep all around the pitch on Paradise to cheer on our heroes: Stan Woodgett in goal, George Lawrence, Cliff Yearn, Ernie Barraclough, Ted Deards, Tommy Joyce, who kept 'The Chequers' pub, Danny McCusker, Jack Lockwood, Ken Pope, Albert Butcher, they were as well known to us as First Division players, better, in fact.

Later we followed the exploits of the great cup winning team under professional coach George King, with Arthur Morgan in goal, the mighty Tony Green of the cannon-ball shot, Norman South, Frankie Oliver, Ron Hunter, Bobby Shields, Ken Pope, Mo Hipkin. Peter Chaloner, Terry Flatt. They reached the 'First Round Proper of the FA Cup in 1956, the biggest day in Ely City's footballing history and one of the biggest days in my footballing family's history, coming a year before my grandad died. They lost 6 – 2 at home to Torquay in front of 4,000 spectators. It would have been 4000 and 1, but I had to hear about it second hand as I was with the school on a rugby trip to Bedford.

We loved watching the football and the other events organised on Paradise and later I was to go in that old wooden pavilion and get ready for cricket matches, change in those old stable changing rooms for Cricket and Rugby and have tea in the old shack in the corner by Deacon's Lane. I would also play tennis for Ely on the grass courts there in the corner next to Rickwood's orchard (where the Paradise Pool now stands), but that was a few years ahead. I can't remember going on Paradise when I was a child except for an organised event. Any adult or child attempting to go on there at any other time faced the wrath of the formidable groundsman, Mr Frumant.

The Park was a favourite playground for the Broad Street children. The main Park that is, not the Dean's Meadow; that was strictly forbidden.

An iron sheep fence ran alongside the path with a wicket gate at each end. It was all rough pasture with buttercups and daisies, except for the Choir School cricket pitch fenced on the flat grass at the bottom of Cherry Hill – another no-go area. Cattle grazed the park.

In Victorian times there was a promenade path all around the Park, which revealed startlingly different views of the cathedral and the surrounding countryside from the top of Cherry Hill.

We went to the Park for conkers from the horse chestnut trees in autumn. Walnut trees attracted attention as well. There were two in the park and the stump of one remains on the corner of the cricket pitch. Its nuts were always wizened in the shell.

Another tree, long gone, on the right slope of Cherry Hill bore more succulent nuts.

The prize ones were, however, in the Dean's Meadow; French walnuts, so they said. The braver element among the boys would go after them to the wrath of the groundsman. Retribution came swiftly. In particular, the Headmaster of Silver Street Boys' School caned, without fear or favour, any lad found with the telltale brown stains from walnut skins on his hands.

In winter, when the snow fell, we took our home-made sledge to the Park. Happy memories of whizzing down the hill, swerving to avoid the solitary cherry tree half way down the slope or of German POWs stamping out a ski run, then, flexing their knees and swooping down on their studded boots.

From the 1952 Guide to the City of Ely

The River

'Roswell' was on high ground and behind the house the land kept sloping away. Sometimes I would explore beyond the end of the field. Across the fields led me to Springhead Lane and from there across the railway line, to the road leading up to the Great Ouse River Board workshops. There were pits with half sunken boats and barges, old railway trucks rusting away and a smell, a strong smell of diesel, mixed with the river smells.

Cuckoo Bridge was a swaying rickety wooden bridge, leading to a path near the settling ponds, an area frequently warned about. I never went near them. The very name was frightening and stories of children drowning in the still deep waters were impressed on my young mind.

It was an adventure though as the path turned and opened up and the gaunt Meccano like structure of the iron bridge came into view. My father enjoyed taking walks that way and once when I was still quite young I walked and walked, over Cuckoo Bridge, over the Iron Bridge, along the track by the River, past the Sugar Beet factory, over the railway crossings in Queen Adelaide, round by Thistle Corner, up the Common and eventually, after several hours, home, worn out.

The Pits again were a forbidden area. There dark still waters were deep and dangerous, and even had I been a swimmer, I would not have tested them.

Before the deep water dredging to improve floodwater control, there were paddling places all along the river. There was one about halfway along the Cresswells (pronounced Creesulls), but my favourite place was by the High Bridge where the arms of the old bridge foundations made a little cove. We played there for hours with little tiddler nets made from old stockings.

I loved to find the freshwater mussel shells when we were paddling. With their pale greenish brown outside and iridescent inside, they sparked dreams of finding a freshwater pearl in the gravel.

On the wash beside the High Bridge, all my childhood, there was a very deep oblong pit, well fenced with barbed wire to keep the unwary out. No one swam in there.

Hot weather drew people to the river. We thought nothing of jumping in off the High Bridge.

At Littleport we had galas in the river at Sandhill Bridge and they dived off the bridge. I was never brave enough to dive – it was bad enough making contact with the muddy bottom and what lurked there, probably old bicycles, with your feet, let alone your head.

There were several more paddling places all along the White Bank towards Newmarket Bridge. You could paddle out quite a long way without getting out of your depth.

It's a different tale now, straight in up to your waist, two steps and you are over the edge. All in a good cause to keep the flood waters at bay, but nowhere near as much fun.

We had barges on the river, not the decorated narrow boats we see now, which are a fairly recent innovation. Wider, flat-bottomed, cumbersome, these barges brought the great sacks of barley to the Maltings and grain to the large barn called the Granary, which stood next to Appleyard's boatyard until the 1960's. I can only remember the old barges mouldering away in the pits.

They were replaced by huge metal monsters which were only used to transport the gault dug in the pits to mend the banks.

A string of barges with a tug pulling had a distinctive sound. The barges banged and clanged against each other. The chains joining them rattled as they negotiated the Cutter bend.

A man would run along and release the chains on the near side. Can you imagine the expression on the face of a modern boat owner if that happened these days?

The 'Rajah' and the 'Pattie' were both familiar sights on the river being used for boating and fishing trips. I can remember going on a friend's birthday treaty in the 'Rajah'.

What possesses the fishermen to hog the path by the *Cutter Inn* where there is hardly room to swing a cat, let alone cast a line? Is it some form of agoraphobia or just keeping an eye on the car?

'The Cutter' and the 1947 floods photographed by W. Martin Lane (by kind permission of The Cambridgeshire Collection'.

Now, I liked fishing. The *Cutter* wall and steps, before the Riverside Walk was constructed, were for after school. The real fishing was along the White Bank from the High Bridge to Newmarket Bridge and beyond to Rat's Island.

Not that I ever caught very much; a few bobby ruffs, a golden-finned perch or two, wriggling eels which curled up your arm and left a trail of slime. I fell in a time or two and came home wrapped in dad's vest clinging to the seat on the back of his bike.

Then there was the bread bait. I can smell it now and taste it.

You could sit with your wellies in the water surrounded by reeds and yellow iris. An odd moorhen paddled across the river, dragonflies hovered while you watched a float fashioned from a goose quill.

Beats me why today's anglers need all the foul weather gear to sit on a gravel path. They would be all right in their slippers.

In wintertime I can understand the attraction of a nice warm hostelry close by. But in summer? It's like and obstacle course with all the expensive equipment laid out: the long poles and the pike rods.

And do they catch anything? It's years since I saw anyone actually land a fish.

My grandad was a keen fisherman. In the hall at 'Roswell' is a case containing a stuffed fish. For years I thought it was a pike but, in fact, it is a tench. It was caught in Roswell Pits in September 1922 with a size 14 hook and it weighed 4lbs 14oz. It's a splendid fish.

Do you remember the 'Sheffielders?' Not that they all came from Sheffield by any means. This was the annual influx of fishermen, their wives and families, from the industrial towns of the north-east midlands for their yearly fishing holiday.

The attics of *The Angel* were full and over-flowing; the *Cutter* was packed. Up and down the streets back bedrooms were pressed into service for bed and breakfast guests. Friendships were forged that lasted a lifetime. Everywhere you heard the boisterous northern voices. 'Eee –lye' they called us.

In the morning they would set off along the banks and sit all day enjoying the fishing and the peaceful rural riverside in stark contrast to the steel mills and factories of their everyday life.

In the evenings they filled the pubs or sat round their hosts' table swapping fishing yarns. A friend found their company so wearing she would creep out to the scullery and read a book behind the copper for five minutes peace and quiet.

They came by bus and train. I think I can remember, as late as 1970, a coach delivering its weekly load of fishermen and waiting at the end of Annesdale for the previous week's passengers.

All gone. They come by car now, just for the day, mostly from London judging by the club badges.

Grandad would come into the kitchen at 'Roswell' with a metal container, slapping with water and fish. The fish were tipped flapping and flipping into the large sink. They brought the smell of the river with them and after they were killed, cleaned and fried, they brought the taste of the river too. Very bony and not like fish in fish and chips was what I remember.

The 'Swim Through Ely' was the event of the year. Men and boys started from the Newmarket Bridge; women and girls from the Old Bathing Place. It attracted swimmers from far and near. A Granta (Cambridge Town Swimming Club) man was usually the overall winner, but Ely had the trophies for local swimmers, not that I ever won anything.

The women would be off and out of sight, the men pounding up behind, while the rest of us straggled along. Swans were a hazard. You have no idea how big a swan looks coming towards you, wings spread, when you are actually in the water. It's no help when spectators throw stones hoping to deflect the bird. It only makes it more angry and all you can do is duck under the water and hope the swan keeps going.

It was a filthy business really. The river was not as polluted as it is today, but the black fen soil is suspended in the water and you come out looking like a chimney sweep.

There was a Gala in the evening. There were speed races across the river and water polo. This was men only, but I did once play in goal, when they were desperate. The goal posts were fixed to the huge horse chestnut trees standing on the other side of the river and to the landing stage on this side. It was great fun, but I can still remember standing on those gnarled roots under water and imagining them dragging me down.

Sometime towards the end of the War, my memory has the Boat Race being held on the Ouse near Littleport. We went to watch it and I caused a minor sensation by running down the bank towards the river much to the alarm of my parents and others. At one point I remember feeling that my legs might be running away with me, but I stopped short of plunging into the cold water. That is all I recall apart from the crowds and the excitement.

When I was older I collected the autographs of some of the crews when they came to train at Ely. As small boys we were thrilled by the sight of these huge athletes. We didn't get much excitement and without television we were not blasé about such things. The University crew training in Ely was an event and they were stars. In one splendid set of signatures from 1951 there is 'J.G.P. Crowden', distinguished oarsman, businessman and now Lord Lieutenant.

Fenmen were famous for their skating abilities. With the characteristic figure bent double, arm behind the back, speeding across the ice they took on all comers.

I had an old pair of Fen Runners, steel blades set in flat wooden pattens, strapped to my shoes, but I couldn't really skate properly and never aspired to the much desired Norwegian skates.

I do, however, remember a moonlight night, when my dad took me down to the Wash on the left by the High Bridge, where the ice stretched clear to Newmarket Rail Bridge, give or take the odd tussock of grass.

I crouched down and hung on to one end of my new, hand-knitted, High School scarf. He towed me at high speed along the Wash towards the Old Bathing Place. The scarf stretched and stretched. We were not very popular when we returned home.

Do you remember the zing of a pebble thrown across the ice and the air bubbles floating below the black ice? But make sure you stick to the Washes and mind the dykes. 'If she cracks, she bears; if she bends, she breaks', as they say, and never ever go on the river; it's deep and it's dark and it's deadly.

From the 1952 Guide to the City of Ely

School Days

"Now the holidays are over,
Back to school we come,
First a bunch of flowers for teacher,
Then we sit and do a sum."

Early steps in poetry at Market Street Infants School.

The reception class was the right-hand door opening straight off the street, nearly opposite the large open fire with its sturdy iron fireguard. Our first task consisted of threading a coloured shoelace through the holes in a punched card. We had small blackboards and chalk, not slates, and boards for smelly plasticine.

Miss Day taught us. Round the walls were placards with the alphabet and simple words such as cat, dog and characters in our reading books. One rejoiced in the name of Old Lob. Have you ever heard of anyone called Lob?

After a couple of terms we were divided, some to Miss Knight at the bottom of the playground and the others to Miss Winchester's class. I went to Miss Winchester and she had a fascinating way of drawing. She would slide the blue chalk lengthways along the top of the board for the sky and the green along the bottom for the grass, yellow for sand, brown for earth and draw a house or a boat in the middle. It didn't do to waste chalk, or anything else in wartime.

A sheet of exercise paper was torn into eight, sums, as they were called, were worked from cards in pencil and rubbed out time and time again until the paper disintegrated. Not that I had any trouble with sums. Along the closed piano lid was laid a length of linen fashioned into pockets and numbered in wool embroidery from one to ten. There were perhaps half a dozen cards in each pocket and you had to do sums on each and get them right, before you could take another card. When each pocket had been worked you could go on to the next.

PE was called Drill. Out in the walled playground we were divided into four teams wearing red, blue, green and yellow sashes. For some reason no one ever wanted to be in the yellow team, but as far as I can remember teams were chosen at random.

Most of Drill was running on the spot, arms stretch, knees bend with a few team games at the end. When it was dry and warm in summer it was a great treat to get the mats out. On oval raffia striped mats we could lay in the sun doing forward rolls and handstands. I never managed a proper handstand without collapsing.

There was no PE kit or plimsolls. The girls just tucked their dresses in their knickers and the boys all wore short trousers anyway.

Empire Day was at the end of May. On that day Miss Hazel would march us out into the playground each clutching a faded flag from pre-war days. Two of the biggest children would stand in the centre supporting a much larger flag on a pole.

We would then all march round singing: "And up with the flag of old England, the flag of the brave and true. From lands far away men are calling today, three cheers for the red white and blue."

On the wall of the classroom, a map liberally coloured in red showed the extent of the Empire from Canada and the Caribbean in the West to Hong Kong in the East, South to Africa, India, Australia, New Zealand and chains of Pacific islands.

Completely ignoring the fact that many places were in enemy hands in the Far East. They were all our responsibility, to be looked after we were told. The fact that many of them did not want to be looked after any more and would opt out the minute they got the chance did not come into it. Somehow it was all tied up with Sunday School and missionaries and we must look after the children.

Every now and then the air raid siren would go and we were marched to the shelter, where we crouched waiting for the Luftwaffe. We shared the shelter with the evacuee mothers from the Grange Nursing Home. Had one of the babies decided to arrive in the middle of a raid, it would have brought a whole new dimension to education in those prim and proper days.

The first school I went to was Market Street Infants School. To a five year old it was a large, high building, formal and full of hidden terrors. On my first day I was somewhat surprised to find that other children were crying; it seemed the appropriate thing to do and I cried as well.

My father had woken me that morning. 'You start school today,' he'd said.

'How long will I have to go to school?' I asked.

'About ten years,' he'd replied.

'I don't think I'll stick it,' was my often recalled reply.

Miss Hazel was the Headmistress and I remember Miss Winchester. The main body of the school was a large high hall with a wooden and glass divider half way along its length. There was a room to the right of the entrance along the front of the building and a smaller room at the far end. There were toilets and cloakrooms to one side on the way to the walled playground. I recall on one occasion coming back into the main building and one of my companions pointing out with some glee a cane hanging up above the door.

School began the Term after you turned five. I remember the first Term I was there that there was a general election. Many of the children were sent to school wearing ribbons or rosettes in party colours: Conservative pink, Liberal blue or Labour red.

Occasionally a box of books was produced and we had a short time to choose a book. Most of them were small green covered books. Mine I think was Greek Myths and Legends chosen in desperation as I had to hurry. I was disappointed with my choice, it was a dull, worn book, I much preferred the bright comics that I learnt to read with, but I was a reader, so I read.

I remember a special occasion when we put on a display of dancing in the presence of the Canon Rowsell, the Vicar at St Mary's Church, and other notables. I was too shy to ask a girl to partner me, so I was teamed with a boy and he went wrong so we had to be withdrawn from the floor in case we wrecked the whole dance.

And that is all I recall of the first two years of my school life. Except I do remember the name of my dancing partner, but since he will blame me for going wrong in that dancing display I wouldn't dream of naming him.

I can vaguely remember being marched in crocodile fashion down Fore Hill from Market Street Infants School to Broad Street Junior Girls. The boys went to Silver Street as there were no mixed schools in those days.

Broad Street School was an L-shaped building with a high-ridged roof and exposed beams. Typical of a Victorian school, the windows were far above the pupils' heads – to stop any staring out – and it was lit by hissing gas jets on dark winter afternoons.

We used steel pen nibs and blue/black ink in little china inkpots about the size of a cotton reel or small glass domes. The ink had a metallic smell, and taste as well, if you licked your fingers.

There were only two classes at Broad Street. We were seven years old and encountered sewing lessons for the first time. Being left-handed was a definite handicap at this point. It was no help in producing the required neat hemstitch. Work became progressively grubbier as it was repeatedly unpicked and resewn. The only way I could get the stitches at the right slant was to hold the cloth upside down when the teacher was looking the other way.

Once the small oblong of linen was hemmed, we had to embroider examples of various stitches in rows like a sampler, fold it in three, make a purse and bring in a length of half-inch tape to serve as a shoulder strap. This was to be embroidered with lazy daisies. There was a war on and I could only get quarter-inch tape.

The teacher was not pleased and made me stitch the whole length in dark brown single chain stitch and spoilt the colour scheme completely.

When the hedgerows are bright with scarlet hips and haws, I remember carefully collecting rose hips to produce syrup for the nation's babies. Older children were given concentrated, pale yellow, very sharp orange juice and the dreaded cod liver oil, which tasted foul.

All this was distributed through the Ministry of Food and, I think, the WVS, to try and keep the children healthy when food was rationed.

There was dried milk for the babies too. We all had milk at school in small bottles, about a third of a pint, sealed by a cardboard disk with a hole in the middle for a straw.

It makes my teeth go on edge even now to think of licking the cream off the cardboard. The little disks were collected and used to wind wool round, making pom poms, or they were covered in raffia and sewn together to make shopping bags.

A real treat came when the milk arrived frozen. The bottles were lined up in the wide, white-washed hearths of the open school fires, inside the fireguards to thaw.

Those close to the fire were warm and sweet, just as if the milk had come straight from the cow. Best of all though were the half thawed ones at the back, the nearest thing to ice-cream we tasted in those dark days.

We had school parties, all girls of course. It was, bring your own sandwiches, cake and a cup with a bit of red cotton round the handle. The food was all mixed up on plates – sardine sandwiches and currant buns, jam sandwiches and fairy cakes. We played *The Farmer's in his Den* and *Squeak, Piggy, Squeak*.

Gone were the days, fortunately, when the left handed were forced to change or be punished for smudging work. My problem was being left-footed as well, especially as the pride and joy of the Headmistress was to teach meticulous country dances.

Through *Strip the Willow*, and *Circassian Circle*, she would slap and slap my right leg until it performed to her satisfaction.

Who says the 'good old days'?

Boys on the left, girls on the right and a wall down the middle so there would be no contact. A typical Victorian church school built at the rear of St Mary's church and Thomas Parson's Square with the entrances on Silver Street. It must have been quite a small school, with an enclosed playground and outside toilets. It was officially called the Ely Voluntary Primary Junior Boys' School, to us it was Silver Street Boys' School.

I was seven and just remember the first classroom around the side of the school. My teacher was Miss Thurmott, the Head teacher was Mr Thrower. My first report , rather alarmingly titled 'Terminal Report', recorded that I was 'Good' at Reading, 'Fair' at Writing, but 'untidy at times', apparently I was 'Very Fair' at Arithmetic and 'Fairly Good' at Drawing. I had missed the Exams, through yet another childhood illness and was placed 32 out of 35. 'Michael could do better – he is inclined to be careless.' Well, that was me at the age of seven, apparently.

By my second year the Headteacher was Mr Dobson, a dark haired, neat-moustached man, who swung the cane with efficiency and regularity. Mrs Dobson was my teacher in that year.

I remember Drill in that small playground and the games we played there, kinds of cricket and football and the quieter games with marbles and cigarette cards.

I recall taking part in a play once on the tiny stage in the school hall. I didn't have a line to say but I did have a small walking stick as a character touch.

When I was about nine or ten, my teacher was Mr Holt. I liked him and he did well by the odd assortment of boys who sat before him. There were Gerard Blackwell and Jack Stanton, whose fathers were both policemen and they lived in the row of police houses next to the Clinic in Downham Road, Barry Staines, from near Cross's shop along Lynn Road, David Blake and Ken Ellingham, both keen footballers and cricketers, Stephen Bishop who came even further than me as he lived up Orchard Estate, Graham Bristow, Derek Bailey, whose father was groundsman at the King's School , Kenny Purchase, Michael Barber, Cyril Austin, David Edwards, Eric Ellingham, who wanted to work on the railway, Michael Taylor, Alfie Wilson, and others, all boys of all sorts of abilities and skills and temperaments, and over thirty in the class.   In my last year our teacher was Mr Teale, who went on to be Headteacher of Prickwillow School until it was closed.

Silver Street School c 1949. Headteacher Mr Dobson,in his gown, with Mr Holt and his boys. Left to right, back row: David Harper, Nunn, Colin Rutterford, Keith Giddens, Tony Ball, Jack Stanton, David Blake, Philip Tuck, Alan Popple; Third row: Maurice Jugg, Michael Payton, Peter Johnson, John Turrell, Michael Rouse, Gerard Blackwell, Brian Cross, Barry Staines, Peter Bush, Stephen Bishop, Graham Bristow; Seated: Derek Bailey, Terry Roberts, Kenneth Purchase, Day, Mr F.J. Dobson, Mr A.K. Holt, Michael Barber, Horace Griggs, Kenneth Ellingham, Cyril Austin; Front row: David Edwards, Eric Ellingham, Michael Taylor and Alfie Wilson.

We were in a classroom tucked away in the far corner close to the church wall. There was a tortoise stove just inside the door. The crate of morning milk would be placed before it in winter, so the bottles nearest got the warmest. How silently we sat, arms folded, straining up in our chairs to be noticed as the quietest, so we could be one of the first to choose – hot, just warm or very cold milk.

Mr Dobson had left to become Headteacher of Witchford Secondary Modern School and our new Headteacher was a Mr Moore, who had been, or was, a first class football referee and brought us in some programmes.

We walked to and from school, that was four trips a day, because we went home for Lunch, about five miles a day in my case. There was a time when if we had a penny halfpenny we would call in the morning at the side widow of Bonnett's Baker's shop, a narrow shop on the corner of Chequer Lane and High Street, and buy half a small new loaf. We would tear still hot chunks off it and eat it as we trailed across Palace Green on the last stage of the walk to school.

The day came, however, that I will never forget. We had sat the 'Eleven plus' exam in the school hall. Three papers I think, English, Arithmetic and a general intelligence paper. It was a desperately anxious time. My father had had to leave school at twelve and find whatever work he could, starting off on the land. His overwhelming ambition was for me to have the education that he had been denied. That meant I had to pass the 'Eleven plus'.

Some weeks later the results were known. I remember arriving in the doorway of the classroom and seeing a small group of some of my friends in the middle of the room. They looked towards me, enquiringly. I nodded, they smiled. I'd passed and I joined them.

A much larger group of boys were muttering that they didn't want to go to that 'snobs' school anyway', that Needham's had been good enough for their father and that's where they wanted to go. It was the great dividing moment between the handful of us who passed and the large majority who didn't. That's how we saw it. We didn't know euphemisms about 'selection for the most suitable school'. You either 'passed' or 'failed'.

At one time nearly all children went to Sunday School whether or not their parents attended church or chapel. Sent would be a better word, no one I knew was given the choice.

I started off at the Primitive Methodist Chapel in Victoria Street, as I have recalled, but when I was old enough, as I was really Church of England, I joined the Sunday School at St Mary's Church. The boys sat on the left, girls on the right. Just before it started a group of boys in grey flannel suits and hob-nailed boots were marched in from the Remand Home across the street. The girls from the children's home in the *Chantry* came too and the boys from the home behind the Tower.

We were given stamps with Bible pictures on them to stick in attendance books. Has anyone still got theirs? They must be museum pieces now.

In the afternoon a Sunday School for 8 – 12 year olds was presided over by Miss Willink in the Central Hall. Miss Willink was a formidable but kindly lady, who with her sister had been a missionary in India. Now settled in Ely she was also a leading member of the WVS.

The Sunday school parties were similar to the school parties, while rationing was on, but they were mixed parties which added a certain frisson to *The Farmer wants a Wife* and musical chairs was more of a scrum.

Sunday School Class c.1948 at Snettisham or Heacham

When we were thirteen Miss Willink trained us to take the infant classes run by Miss Trett round in the Trinity Parish Room. We attended preparation classes in the week, where she taught us the lesson for Sunday and showed us how to make a flannel board from an old blanket. First colouring and cutting out Bible figures, palm trees and donkeys. Then sticking lint on the back to be able to move them round the board while telling stories from the Bible.

It was all very simple; we sang a hymn, said our prayers, told the story and then the little ones would draw a picture and take it home to Mum in time for tea.

> "Holiday time is nearly here,
> Sing us a song of the sea,"

47

We warbled with Miss Hazel and Miss Winchester at Market Street Infants School.

However, the war cast a long shadow across our childhood.

I was nine before the beaches were cleared of mines and I saw the sea for the first time on a Sunday School treat to Hunstanton.

All the Sunday Schools went together; a whole train was chartered. On arrival, the Sunday School superintendent, Miss Willink, set up her deck chair beside the pier.

She planted a flagstaff in the sand and raised the Union Flag. It was easy to wander off along the tide line and lose your bearings, but we could always find Miss Willink.

At first sight it was a bit disappointing. Where was the sea? Where were the waves? Golden sand as far as the eye could see, stranded fish, razor shells, cockle shells.

Eventually the tide lapped lazily in, filling the sand castle moat we were not too old to dig. We had a lot of time to catch up on.

Tea on trays for the grown-ups, and American cream soda from under the pier for us. It tasted like nectar.

Then came the trauma of catching the train home, with everyone milling around the station concourse. I was always convinced we would get on the wrong train, but we never did.

Tired, our faces glowing with the wind and the sun, we would stagger home shoes full of sand. We had seen the sea at last.

> "I am the child of God
> I ought to do His will
> I can do what he tells me
> And by His Grace I will"

*A prayer taught to us by Miss Willink. I think she had written it. She **was** the Sunday School as I remember it. She is a person very dear to my memories of childhood and had a great influence over my behaviour.*

Never to be forgotten was the train excursion to Hunstanton and Miss Willink with her base camp and the union flag. What a treat even for me who had seen the sea before and at Hunstanton too.

I remember classes in St Mary's Church and the old man who came in to pump the organ. There were classes at Trinity Parish Room conducted by Miss Trett and the older girls, like Ann Harding, and later classes at the Central Hall with Miss Willink, Miss Knights and Mr Lee, when I was eleven or twelve and became a 'teacher' to a small group of younger pupils.

Miss Willink, would take her dog, rumoured to be a relation of the 'real' Lassie, and a small group of us children to collect money for charity from the queues going into the 'Rex Theatre' for a Lassie film – and long queues they were too.

September 1948 I stood on the pavement outside Bedford House in St Mary's Street, a very new High School girl. In navy blue beret with a bright yellow badge, a three pleat gym slip, navy and yellow striped tie and probably the regulation gaberdine mac. A spanking new leather satchel from Blakeman's shop and shoes polished to please a sergeant major.

Eventually a teacher came out and herded the new girls into the school. The Headmistress, Miss Tilly, was away on a sabbatical in Rome, studying her beloved Etruscans. Her place was taken by the equally formidable steely-eyed, Miss Defew.

The preparatory school must have closed that year because we had two of the pupils in with us. One still had the old blue felt school hat with elastic under the chin, and a straw one for summer. The school had expanded to accommodate the influx of scholarship girls after the 1944 Education Act. In the playground a row of concrete prefabs stretched along the wall. About 80 new girls were divided into three classes – A, Alpha and Remove. As Lower IIIA, we were shown into the end prefab with Miss Mahony as form mistress. Sitting on the south side by the window in the sun, it was difficult to keep awake some hot summer afternoons when things droned on a bit. That was the only time I ever got into trouble, for yawning. I had to go and stand outside the staff room in the main building and apologise to the teacher concerned.

The cloakrooms were so over-crowded, the whole class shared pegs in what was no more than a cupboard. Girls from all the villages way out in the fens as far as Lakenheath and Mildenhall travelled each day.

The cookery and needlework rooms were housed in the wooden huts behind Bedford House proper, just across from the bowed window of the Music room. Reached by an open covered walk from the main cloakrooms, they were built of planks of tarred wood; very hot in summer and freezing in winter. You entered the needlework room and turned left into the cookery room furnished with long tables, sinks, draining boards and cookers.

I did not become over-familiar with this room; I only had two cookery lessons.

The first was to make rock buns. We were sent home with a list of ingredients required: flour, sugar, margarine and an egg. Remember this was 1948 and rationing was still in force. This was probably my own ration for a week.

I was quite keen for a start, but when it came to adding the liquid to produce the required consistency, I overdid it. As all good cooks will know rock buns have to be quite a stiff mix to hold together on a baking sheet; mine didn't.

The teacher scooped the mess up into a half-dozen bun tin and plonked it in the oven where they rose into quite respectable currant buns. When I took them home, mother was not impressed. She could have made a dozen from that amount.

The next week it was plain biscuits. Mine were not perfect but adequate; however, a classmate saw fit to play catch with them and missed. The bag of biscuits shattered on the floor and that was the end of my culinary education.

Ely High School Vth Form 1953

The next week a teacher shortage meant we had to choose between Geography and Domestic Science. I leapt at the chance and never looked back.

So there we were being given the chance of a lifetime: Classics, Mathematics, Science and Languages. I do wish someone had explained what phonetics were before we launched into French accent, and what Nominative Vocative, Accusative represented before we started Latin. I was hopeless at languages, it came as a great relief when, because of staff shortages again, we had to choose between French and Geography in the Lower Fourth.

All our games lessons were held on Paradise. We probably got more exercise trailing back and forth for netball and hockey in the winter and rounders and tennis in the summer, than actually playing.

We had to walk everywhere in crocodile. All the way down to the swimming pool in Angel Drove in summer. That was a pretty chilly affair too and I was used to it. What it was like for non-swimmers shivering around in the shallow end, I hate to think. At least I could plough backwards and forwards to keep my circulation going.

Then it was getting dressed in the draughty, unheated cubicles and a chilly plod back up the hill with wet hair. If I was lucky and it was just before dinner, I could get permission to break ranks and nip home to Broad Street and a nice warm kitchen.

I wasn't so keen on gymnastics but found the gym hall fascinating; straight out of all the books we used to read in those days about girls' boarding schools and the adventures they had. There were wall bars, ropes, parallel bars, vaulting horses and fat heavy coconut mats to land on. Strangely enough you took your gymslip off and tucked your blouse in your navy blue knickers for that, just like at junior school. But I never managed to climb to the top of a rope and write my name on the beam in the dust.

As a result of having passed the 'Eleven plus' and satisfactorily coming through an interview, I had been awarded a county scholarship; I would be a day pupil at the King's School and not going with many of my friends to Soham Grammar School.

So, six years after the war had ended, some rationing still in force and I'm standing self-consciously, school cap perched on my head, school blazer and grey short trousers, all purchased from Butteriss' in Ely High Street, brand new leather satchel, bought from Thurmott's in Market Street, with Jack Stanton, Eric Ellingham and possibly some other new day boys, somewhere in the small roadway near the gate to the Headmaster's House. No one has told us where to report but eventually we must have been rescued and introduced to our new school, or rather our new school was introduced to us. No one could have felt more alone in those early days than I did.

I was a 'new bug' and a day boy and there was a whole big secret world of a boarding school with its rituals, mysteries and friendships that was a closed book to me and remained so for most of my days at King's.

I only realise now that it must have been quite a small school, perhaps fewer than 200 boys? There was the Choir School, Priory House, the Headmaster's House and Hereward as boarding houses. But even to dayboys it was an all-consuming experience controlling every evening with homework and all day Saturday. It took some adjusting to the regime. For the start of my second year I went into long trousers and not long after, being nearly six feet tall, I persuaded the powers that were that I should be allowed to stop wearing a cap. It looked 'like a pimple on a round of beef', as we used to say.

I remember fragments. I enjoyed taking part in plays. The first one I did was 'Toad of Toad Hall'. I was Chief Stoat, and there were so many of us Wildwooders that we waited behind a screen alongside the audience upstairs in the Porta. Later in other productions like 'She Stoops to Conquer' and 'The Government Inspector' I remember a hut on the flat roof above where the Franklins' lived, and we waited in there.

The Porta was where we saw films like 'The Card', 'The Man in the White Suit' and 'The Ghost Train'. We waited crushed in the small lobby downstairs. There was a pungent smell of sulphur coming from the boiler and it coated the mouth and left a strong taste alleviated at times in the interval by an orange flavoured chocolate ice cream. The projector and films came from George Jefferson, the printer, on St Mary's Street, who produced the local 'bible','The Red Book', the directory to who lived where in Ely. It's strange thinking back that at the time Ely had three cinemas and I still went and saw a number of films in those shows at the Porta. It was to the 'Rex Cinema' in the centre of Ely, however, that the whole school went in 1953 to see a matinee showing of the Coronation film and 'The Ascent of Everest'.

I smell cabbage boiling and I remember waiting on some small stone steps by a doorway from the undercroft dining hall that led to the Headmaster's study. There was a small window cut in the thick stone walls, but it was a lonely little cell where one waited usually for Mr. Brown to dispense summary justice with the cane. The kitchens were nearby and the smell of cabbage pervaded and the sound of the cooks could be heard rattling around in some mysterious area. I wanted to be with them in their noisy clattering environment with the cabbages, not where I was nervously standing.

Mr Brown moved on to Bedford School and was replaced by Mr Fawcett with his close cut white hair, short bristling moustache and florid face.

There was Mr Wilkinson whom I liked because he taught English and loved cricket and I enjoyed both; Miss Arber was a gracious lady teaching Geography to some fairly ungracious boys; there was Mr Osmond, assisted by the elderly Mr Gann, battling against the odds of old laboratories, ancient equipment and in my case a lack of interest in anything scientific. Mr Jones rattled through everything mathematical, while Mr Saunders was exasperated by my failure to cope with Latin. Mr Russell, who always called me 'Roose', put us through our paces in the gym and on the river rowing. There was also Albert Marshall, the general handyman and caretaker and Les Bailey, who looked after the grounds and prepared the cricket wicket, as well as umpiring matches.

In truth the staff were as much a mystery as the whole process I was going through. In the Fifties nothing or no one was ever questioned in authority. The school knew best, so you never mentioned the canings or any other miseries. The prefects could cane harder than most masters and seemed in some cases to enjoy it. They were an elite not to be challenged, but to be feared.

Games afternoons were three times a week on the school field and the Campus. At one time a new rugby field was established over Angel Drove opposite the Campus, but the experiment didn't last long. Tennis was played on the Theological College courts. Cross-country runs took us down Back Hill, along the drove by the river, over the iron bridge, alongside the Beet Factory settling ponds, over rickety Cuckoo Bridge, across the railway line, down Springhead Lane, along the cinder track between the allotments and back through Bull Lane, Broad Street and up Back Hill past Horace Partridge's patriotically painted (for the Coronation) red, white and blue cottage, to finish outside the Porta.

There was an activity afternoon for cadets and scouts. I was a scout and through scouting got my first chance to go on camping holidays, unforgettable adventures to the Peak District and Lake District among other places. Our leader in the Peak District was Mark Coe, later to become a Colonel in the army and to be murdered by the IRA in Germany. Later our scout-master was the precentor of the cathedral, the Rev. Edward Longford, who would drill us up and down the College.

I remember the grey shadow of the cathedral looming over much of our lives, the humming coldness of the Lady Chapel and morning assemblies. I cycled to and from school and if I was late some mornings, I would hurl my bicycle against the railings around St Cross Green and rush down the path, hoping that the hymn had not started. I remember, too, the inside of the lantern tower full of scaffolding as the battle was fought against death watch beetle.

I remember Matron, surrounded by piles of laundry, dispensing small bottles of milk to day-boys at break; the anxious craning at the notice boards near the dining hall to look at teams, results and to find out what was going on.

There are other fragments: buying penny cream buns from a small Co-op shop in Silver Street; cramming muddy bodies into the murky water of a large concrete bath in the dayboys' changing room after games; the coldness (again) of the public open air unheated swimming pool near the gasworks, and, when older, Saturday night dances to records in the Library with those rare objects of desire, girls.

From the 1952 Guide to the City of Ely

Around the City

The Corn Exchange stood in the corner of the Market Place facing the fish and chip shop. It had a row of columns along the front and looked like the Court building in Lynn Road.

Its main function was as a Corn Exchange on Thursdays. Around the walls were fixed desks and stalls with names of the various corn merchants and dealers. Children were not, as far as I can remember, allowed in.

I had an uncle from Huntingdon way, who dealt in hay and straw, who turned up regularly on market days. I have a vague recollection of the market bars in the hotels being quite important in the process of dealing.

The Tuesday furniture sales were far more important to us. During the war household items were in short supply and it was a source of rare entertainment.

At a table set high on a platform, Mr Comins sat with his clerk, commanding the proceedings like an emperor. A long table was set between rows of chairs and forms where the more fragile items, china and ornaments, were displayed.

Formidable ladies sat in their accustomed seats in the front row and the rest of us crowded in behind. Woe betide the mother whose baby cried or child chattered, she was ordered out. If the ladies gossiped during the bidding Mr Comins would bang with his gavel to silence them.

In the late autumn there was a toy sale. Such excitement to see so many toys. I still have the remains of a tea set bid for there. Cups like strawberries on leaf-shaped saucers. I saw a set in Bethnal Green Children's Museum recently, labelled '1900

When I was a child every Thursday market day my grandad had a trade stand in front of the Corn Exchange on Ely Market Place. The lorry would be loaded up in the works or yard the night before and first thing in the morning they would trundle the half a mile or so into the centre of Ely and set up. There was a shed on wheels, known as 'the office', which stood with its back to the front of the Corn Exchange opposite Lancaster's Fish and Chip Shop and the derelict face of the old 'Temperance Hotel'. His display of cattle cribs, ladders, gates and sheds would be set out in front of him, ideally placed to catch the farmers as they moved from the Cattle Market through the 'White Hart Inn' archway to the Corn Exchange.

There he stood hearing all the news and doing some business. Uncle Herbert Roythorne, his brother in law, with the waxed moustache, and watch chain stretched across his ample waistcoat, would join him to pass the time of day. Grandma and mum would use the office as their base for shopping, steadily placing bags there as they visited their regular stalls. My father, by then out of the RAF after becoming a Sergeant in the police Special Investigation Branch stationed at Duxford, had resumed his pre-war work as an Insurance Agent and would be back and forth from the Liverpool Victoria Offices on the Fore Hill, where the smiling Tom Mann sat in the main office with the various secretaries and clerks. Everybody met up at Grandad's 'office', without it the market was unthinkable.

I would arrive later in the afternoon from school, and try, in summer, to get myself treated to an ice cream cornet from Pocklington's van and then head off to look at the comics on Thornton's stall. It was there in the early 1950's I started buying 64 page fully illustrated, in black and white, pockets books in a Thriller Comics Library series. Here were stories by Edgar Wallace and Sapper, but also the classics like 'Jane Eyre' and 'The Three Musketeers'. Through these and the coloured American Classics Illustrated I learnt the stories and read 'the classics'.

A typical Thursday tea time would see me curled up in a chair with a comic book from the market and fresh fish for tea off one of the stalls.

Hands up all those who were an errand boy or girl. Every shop I can think of had one or two youngsters to run errands. Not just the grocers, butchers and fishmongers, but the cobblers, the chemists, dress shops, men's outfitters and ironmongers as well.

Saturdays and after school they buzzed around the town and out to the nearby villages. I delivered the Sunday joints to Stuntney for Newson's Butchers.

An acquaintance worked for Gardiners, the Chemist, in High Street, next to Burrows. One of his errands was to deliver prescriptions to the Isolation Hospital behind the Tower Hospital.

The matron was concerned because he never spoke. He just rushed in, handed over the package and rushed out. She enquired of Mr Gardiner, could the boy not speak?

Mr Gardiner took him to task and the lad had to admit that he was petrified of catching something like scarlet fever or diptheria. So, when he reached the door, he would take a deep breath and hold it until he was safely outside again.

A generation before my father worked for the International Stores at the top of Fore Hill. Sweets and biscuits were not packaged in those days. Biscuit tins were fitted with glass lids for display purposes along the front of the counter and sweets were displayed in open boxes.

A crafty errand boy could snatch a treat as he passed through the shop. Harry's mistake was to snatch a fondant sweet which stuck and melted in his throat. By the time he reached the warehouseman in the back of the shop he was choking and frantically miming the required slap on the back. Fortunately the thump dislodged the sweet – or I would not be here to tell the tale.

Sometimes mother would send me down to a yard in Waterside. This was not my territory and as such was a strange rather frightening area of houses and cottages that had seen better days. There were pubs, brewery buildings and a wide road that ended at the broad slow flowing river. The yard was on the left (where Osier Close is now) and there was a rag and bone man. Mother re-used most things and was a very careful manager. She had to be as money was always tight. She would make peg rugs, save any useful pieces of wrapping paper, and, of course, had a string bag in the 'glory hole' into which went any useful lengths of string. My sister still has the bag and is quite sure that it contains some of mother's original pieces of string! But when she did have some unwanted rags, I would take a bundle of old clothes and rags down to Waterside and hurry away with a few pennies.

I can remember two coal merchants in Ely, Bowgen and Peachey and Coote and Warren, as well as the Co-op in Barton Square.

Coote and Warren were near the railway gates. I have a feeling there was always a coalyard there with a dock leading to the river where coal was off-loaded into barges for the pumping engines, but that was before my time. The Sea Cadets stored their boats there before it was filled in by Standen Engineering.

Bowgen and Peachey were in Jubilee Terrace and, like Coote and Warren, had to off load coal from wagons in the goods yard by the time I worked there. I was more familiar with coal trucks than most young females. I had to do the stock reports.

Every day I had to record the trucks on hand in the yard and at North Junction noting if they were full or empty. Recipients had two days to empty their wagons and after that Demurrage was charged at about half a crown a day. (twelve and a half pence).

Demurrage was the bane of my life and the coal merchants hated it. When the bills went out I would dread the knocking on the goods office hatch; they would even push it up themselves if I wasn't quick enough to answer.

There would be a black-faced coalman, red-rimmed eyes, flat cap over one ear, clutching a grubby bill, insisting a particular truck had been emptied in under two days and the yard foreman had got it all wrong or I had made a mistake. Fortunately the chief clerk would take over at that point, but not before we were all covered in coal dust.

We walked everywhere. As a small schoolboy I walked to school, home again at lunchtime, back to school and then home again.

The walk from Prickwillow Road to Market Street School took me past the junction of Bray's Lane near the busy sweet-smelling Jam Factory, past a tiny dark shed-like shop owned by a Mr Lowe which stood almost opposite my dear Aunt Ada's little cottage squeezed endways onto the road. Further along the road from Aunt Ada's was Croot's little fish and chip shop.

Past Lowe's shop and there was Alp's radio and bicycle shop, where in the workshop at the back Mr Cross would sort out any problems we had with our bicycles, next to Alps' was the 'Majestic' and a chance to look at the posters and displays advertising the films that week.

The 'Majestic' cinema

On the opposite side of the road was 'old' Mrs Alps' shop. From there we would often see her set out in her pony and trap. In a cottage just the other side of the 'High Flyer' lived my friend Michael Dyos.

There was a small wooden butcher's shop before reaching Rickwood's furniture shop on the corner with Newnham Street. Rickwood's Arcade (now the Atrium Club) was where mum and dad furnished their house, right down to the coal scuttle. On the other corner Trinity Parish Room was where I went to Sunday School. Halfway along Newnham Street was the entrance to the Cattle Market with its auction rings and pens, always bustling with activity and the smell of animals on a Thursday. On the other side of the entrance was the 'White Hart Tap' and I remember the Tedora girls who lived there and did a lot of swimming.

Walking past the little dirt lane at the rear of 'The Rex Theatre' that led to the Women's Institute Hall and a builder's yard, the cinema smell lingered in the air.

Once I'd crossed the road, the 'Woolpack' stood on the corner with Market Street and then it was a straight dawdle past Thurmott's leather shop, where we could get our leather football pumped up and laced up, the Central Hall, where we went to parties and celebrations, and not a moment too soon, to school.

I think we came to the end of an era in 1998. The last farmyard within the city – on Lynn Road – was closed.

It always gave me a great deal of pleasure to see the cattle there in the winter months. On frosty days the steam would rise from their curly coats and muzzles as they chewed the cud.

Barton Farm is long gone, swallowed up by the golf course and the King's School. Other farm houses have been absorbed or demolished, on Fieldside, St John's Road, Downham Road and West Fen Road.

Certainly well into the Fifties there was a farmyard right in the middle of Market Street beside the barber's and the cows were taken through the streets to be milked each day. There was another farm down Waterside, just before the antiques warehouse, you can still see the stables.

The Council horses were stabled in Silver Street, I think. Where you go into the car park on foot there is an old stable building with the brick floor of the stable yard. In earlier times it would have been for the army horses when the Militia was there.

Along by the High Bridge was a small-holding with farm buildings and chickens and calves. It was where the marina is now.

There are of course, still cows, calves and cattle over on the washes beyond Babylon, on what someone euphemistically called 'water meadows', when a footbridge across was suggested. It would not do to go wandering about there. You could fall in one of the dykes and never be seen again. Washes were not designed for recreational purposes.

I can never bring myself to buy sprouts until there has been a frost. The same went for celery, although I must admit I buy it all year round now and can live with the Spanish and Israeli versions. But I draw a line at the wishy washy stuff that turns up from California when the shops are desperate.

Nothing really compares with the peppery taste of real black fen white-stalked celery that has been moulded up properly and harvested after a good hard frost.

In the Ely Goods Yard, I watched Cole Ambrose's patient plodding cart horses come jingling under the railway bridge out of the November mists from Stuntney, pulling great creaking orange pink wagons piled high with crates of celery.

The metal-rimmed wheels rumbled up to the loading dock at the station corner of what is now Tesco's car park. The horses would chafe at the bit, stamp, and snort steamy breath into the cold air. It smelled of horses, celery and coal smoke.

Celery was packed straight off the land into crates made of thin strips of pliable wood. These were manhandled into open topped trucks and sent all over Britain.

Italian prisoners of war thought the English were mad to discard the green tops and bore them back to the Cambridge Road camp in great glee for the cookhouse. It has taken nearly half a century for us to follow this sensible example.

On warm summer evenings, along the river, crept the unmistakable whiff of Carmuckle (the Common Muck Hole in Ely-speak). Our part of Ely always had more than its fair share of pungent aromas.

Hall, Cutlack and Harlock's Brewery perfumed the air at the bottom of Fore Hill with a sour, kind of warm Weetabix smell. At the Station Road end, the gas works belched out noxious fumes, which chewed the bricks and stonework of the surrounding buildings.

Half way along Broad Street, Alfred Woods' wood-yard added creosote to the mixture, topped off in winter by the unforgettable, unforgotten sweet muddy tang of the sugar beet factory steaming away at Queen Adelaide.

All gone. The brewery after being Ely Ales, then Steward and Patteson, was gobbled up by Watney Mann and closed at the end of the sixties. The gas works, thankfully, were swept away by the North Sea gas.

The wood-yard modernised and moved down Angel Drove. The Beet factory closed too, but on damp winter days when the wind is in the north, so strong is the smell produced by Wissington factory, it still reaches the city like a ghost from the past.

Childhood was full of smells. Ely was full of smells.

Directly across the Prickwillow Road, of course, was my grandad's workshop with its warm smell of freshly sawn wood and the wonderful rich stinging smell of creosote.

During the 'campaign' in the winter, if the wind was in the right quarter, the sweet smell from the Beet Sugar Factory at Queen Adelaide reached the City and we were not that far from the factory anyway. Even sweeter was the smell from the St Martin's jam factory at the junction of Brays Lane and Prickwillow Road. As children we reliably informed each other that the pips in the raspberry jam were really small wooden chips especially manufactured for the purpose and put into the jam.

Along Station Road there was the unmistakable smell of the gas works. It pervaded the whole area, including the open air swimming pool at the top of Angel Drove.

From the brewery at the foot of Fore Hill the smell of hops and beer flavoured the air. Beer mixed in with the smell of tobacco smoke wafted from the open doors and windows of the many pubs.

From 'The Rex Cinema', the 'Public Room' cinema, but especially from the 'Majestic' cinema at the top of Prickwillow Road, because it was on the edge of the pavement, came that unmistakably pungent, sweet smell of smoke, air freshener and disinfectant.

Shops exuded smells - Thurmott's in Market Street with its rich leather was where we took our leather footballs to be pumped up and have the laces tightened by Mr Thurmott. There was Bennett's the grocers, next to the 'Rex' in Market Street, with the sharp smell of fresh coffee being ground alongside the aroma of cheese being cut and bacon being sliced; from Bonnett's Bakery we could smell fresh bread and from Newstead's wet fish shop in Market Place the cold smell of the sea.

The Ely of my childhood was full of small shops, many of them privately owned with the owners living above the premises. There were several small cold grocery and provision shops like Kays, the Star Supply Stores, Home and Colonial and the Maypole, with its fascinating pictured wall tiles on a level with my childhood nose. I suppose everyone had their regular shops, especially with the wartime rationing. There were several small butcher's shops; Grandma always got her meat from Russell Wright's in the High Street. There was even a cheaper

Peacocks Stores, Kays Modern Food Stores, Bata and Finlay & Co, Tobacconists, High Street, May 1950.

version of Woolworths in Peacocks stores. This was a dark sweet-smelling Aladdin's cave under Coronation Parade in the High Street. Like Woolworths, the goods were set out in sloping wooden trays. I always wanted a 'sorbo' ball. I loved the smell of the multi-coloured rubber skins, concealing solid rubber balls. Some were soft and bouncy, others hard and bouncy and pieces of the ball broke away leaving a black miniature many-cratered moon. The really bouncy ones did tend to hurtle down the street until disappearing, sometimes forever, in a neighbour's hedge or front garden, but how I loved their smell!

Even the Post Office, that bare echoing Victorian building, opposite Bennett's at the top of Market Street smelled of post offices. Was it the glue on the backs of the stamps, ink, letters, red tape, government issue polish? But it was unmistakably 'post office' whatever it was!

Ely's splendid new library is only a few feet from where the first library I can remember was situated.

It was housed in a prefab, somewhere around where the service areas for Tesco's and Waitrose are now. A concrete slab path, open at the sides but with a corrugated iron roof, led to a series of rooms in the prefab hut. In the first you handed over the books you were returning, then in the next room on the right were the shelves of children's books.

It did not take me long to devour what they had to offer, once I was old enough to belong to the library. Enid Blyton's *Famous Five* books and the ones with titles like *The Valley of Adventure* were soon read and the Twins books that took you round the world with Eskimo or African Twins.

I had long since grown out of things like *The Water Babies* and *Peter Pan*. Before long I found my way into the back room and the non-fiction section. My goodness what a treasure trove of travel and real adventure opened up.

My all-time favourite was HV Morton's *In the Steps of the Master* all over the Holy Land between the two World Wars.

Then there were the ones about sailing round Cape Horn or exploring up the Zambesi and the Amazon. I never looked back. I can't even remember where the Fiction section was. Over on the left I suppose.

Not that Mr Picket, the Librarian, would have allowed a child to take any of those. I did go home with *Our Dearest Emma* once which had been misfiled. I had practically finished it by the time someone noticed.

Everywhere there were pubs, small corner shops and shops all privately owned. Trailing back from school along St Mary's Street there was St Mary's Garage and Hotel, then the house of Dr Wells, set back from the road, Jefferson's, the printers, Porter's fruit and vegetable shop, Dr Bamford's house with the surgery round the back, and the shop at Gouldstone's corner, the 'Peacock Inn', the High School buildings, Nice and Co's Garage and the 'King's Arms', where we knew the Wenn family who were distant relations. Mr Gutteridge's hairdressers came next, then Coates, Ladies fashions, and the tobacconist's shop, before Mr Dobson's dark cavern of a gentleman's barbers. Starr and Rignall, where we all went to have our photographs taken, was right on the corner opposite the 'Lamb Hotel'. For a short while just round the corner in the little shop up some steps was a stamp and cigarette card shop. Ah! Now that was my sort of shop as a boy. There were some architects, the Walbro, with its glittering cycles and fascinating radios, the Rural District council offices, Ely Service Motor Co and the 'George and Dragon' on the corner of Chapel Street. The 'King William IV' was on the next corner with Egremont Street. Opposite was Mr Cowley's sweet shop. I would sometimes call in there at the start of the long walk up Lynn Road as I headed home. He also had a stall on Ely market for years.

It wasn't a very interesting walk along Lynn Road to Silver Street school, but we usually mooched along with a few friends, boasting, arguing and generally falling in and out as boys do. Eventually near Nutholt Lane we passed the Beckett family house set back on the corner and the Grange Maternity Home on the other corner. Then came the imposing Court House with the police station up the steps on the right hand side of it. The blue lamp was suspended on a wrought iron entrance arch. We rarely had occasion to go there unless it was to report finding some money or something. Then there was a very solemn moment as the officer came to the front desk and entered whatever it was in an impressive ledger before telling us if it wasn't claimed with in three months it would be ours. The old fire station, by then converted to council officers for the Urban District Council, stood next to the police station. The old gaol was a private house and we crossed Market Street, went past the 'Lamb Tap' and the front of the 'Lamb Hotel'. From there unless we needed to divert to Burrows, it was into Minster Place and the enticing SPCK Bookshop, before turning along Palace Green where the Bishop's Palace was a Red Cross Home for handicapped children , and the last stages of our trek to Silver Street.

I miss the old Eastern Counties buses. Buses should be red. One of our Italian prisoners of war was puzzled by the destination boards. 'Pri-va-te,' he said. 'Where is this place, Pri-va-te?'

Single and double deckers they bounced along the uneven fen roads. Drivers and conductors worked the same routes for years and knew nearly every passenger and where they wanted to get off, even in the pitch dark.

Twice a day they carried the Soham Grammar School boys and the Ely High School girls to and from their separate schools. The railway crossing gates at Ely and Chettisham adding an extra excitement to the day when, being held up at the gates made the pupils late for assembly.

The double-deckers I remember most were called 'low bridge' models, although there were no bridges around Ely high enough to go under. On the top deck these had the gangway at the side which dropped below the level of the seats while passengers sat four to a seat.

It was always a scramble to extricate myself and get down the stairs in time for my stop at the Shade in Soham, where I was living at the time.

The bottom deck was even more hazardous on the side where the gangway above lowered the ceiling. If you stood up without thinking, there was a sharp and painful reminder to lower your head, as indeed the notice on the seat in front of you advised you to do.

Our Doctor was Doctor Beckett in Egremont Street. You just turned up at 9a.m. or 6p.m. and awaited your turn.

The waiting room was narrow with a high ceiling. You sat on slippery bentwood benches or on crackly leather padded ones. There was an assortment of chairs, too, and tall dark cupboards. Boxes on the top had something to do with the doctor's hobby. I was never sure if it was butterfly collecting or insects, but can vaguely remember that he offered a reward for a particular black furry caterpillar.

Medicines were dispensed on the spot, through a hatch in the wall. After a consultation you would wait and soon the hatch crashed up and the medicine was handed through.

Red medicine (iron) for anaemic-looking little girls. White medicine for tummy trouble and an odd greeny yellow translucent one as a 'pick me up'. How the adults fared with serious complaints was never discussed in front of the children. There were mysterious M & B tablets but what for I didn't fathom.

I can only just remember pre-NHS days, but I have seen the doctors bills that came out at 2s 6d (12.5p) for each visit, excluding medicine.

I suppose school, kept an eye on the children's health. 'Nitty Noras' came round regularly and peered in everyone's hair.

A doctor came occasionally and you had to stand around shivering in your underwear on the raffia mats.

It seems entirely possible when you're five or six, that if you put your finger on the large slowly turning cogwheel of a machine for drilling metal that you will be able to stop it.

It must have been a frantic drive from my Uncle's forge in Soham to Ely with my hand wrapped in a blood-soaked towel. Straight to Dr Maurice-Smith's surgery on St Mary's Street. Round the back and into the narrow waiting room and from there straight into his antiseptic smelling room.

I remember going to Market Street School with my finger heavily bandaged and having to hold the teacher's hand in the playground, less my finger should be knocked.

Dr Maurice-Smith saved the end of my finger, it was never the same again, but some things are learnt the hard way.

In addition to putting fingers where they shouldn't be put, falling out of trees, falling off bicycles, getting hit in the face with a cricket bat (one stitch and scarred for life), it seemed the normal misfortune of childhood to catch every illness. Measles, German Measles, more than once, Chicken Pox, Whooping Cough, though I managed to avoid the Mumps.

Whatever it was that had laid me low, Dr Maurice-Smith would come puffing up the stairs to my room, give his verdict in whispered conversation to mum or dad, demonstrate how he could write with both hands at the same time or write a word on my sickly skin before off to his next call.

Everyone, I think, was loyal to their own particular Doctor. They all had separate practices: Dr Maurice Smith, Dr Bamford, Dr Wells, all along St Mary's Street and Dr Beckett in Egremont Street. They lived in some of the largest houses in Ely and were the nearest thing at the time to an aristocracy.

There were several chemists in the town: Gardiners in High Street, next to Burrows, Harrison's next to Steeple Gate, Boots further along the High Street and Sturton and Howard's at the top of Fore Hill

For chesty aches and wheezes a chalky white substance was boiled up on the cooker and while very hot coated all over the chest or back.

A considerable part of childhood seemed to be taken with being 'dosed up'. There was the bright orange juice in the bottles that looked like medicine bottles, the cod liver oil, and for me, an additional brown sticky molasses goo, ladled out by the spoonful.

The School Dental Clinic was in Downham Road. After a visit to the school by the school dentist, those needing treatment were summoned thence.

It had its own peculiar antiseptic smell, not quite like the doctor's surgery or hospital, which I assume was the gas used for extractions.

I can still taste the rubber wedge that kept your teeth apart and the mask that sent you into a dizzy oblivion, only to be revived a few minutes later by far-away voices and a sore gap where the tooth had been.

That did not scare me, but I was not very keen on fillings. Mainly because the drilling machine was operated by the dentist peddling it furiously like a bicycle. When he slowed up, even with an injection of cocaine, it was a bit nerve wracking to say the least.

Our dentist was Mr Taylor, a sports car driving Scot, who worked with Mr Jefferson-Smith. Their practice was in Minster Place at the rear of the Prudential Insurance Offices. We waited downstairs in some trepidation until called up the steep winding stairs to the first floor for treatment. And I remember that too.

I remember organised collections that went on all year for Addenbrooke's Hospital. Although one had to pay to go to the doctor, you did not pay to go to hospital.

Each street had its collector, who would come round once a month, I think, for something like a shilling. (5p), noting it on a little card.

I had my tonsils out in Addenbrooke's annex at the Leys School during the war. We shared the wards with soldiers and airmen who were recovering from injuries. We had cornflakes for breakfast, a bit painful with a sore throat.

Tea shops and snack bars seem to be popping up all over the place. I love to see the pavement cafes. The Buttermarket looks quite continental. What with kebabs, pizzas and American chicken, Indian and Chinese take-aways, it's all a very long way from the days when the Kimberley Cafe and the Woodpecker graced our streets, with the Kum-In café, at the bottom of Cambridge Road, with its wooden tea pot over the door.

The Woodpecker, at the Market Street end of High Street Passage, served the bus passengers with tea and a sticky bun and anyone else who enjoyed a good old fry-up before 'all day breakfasts' were heard of.

Down in Broad Street, the Kimberley Cafe, now the site of the accountants' offices, provided lorry drivers with a bed for the night. The smell of breakfasts of bangers, bacon, fried eggs, bread and beans perfumed the morning air.

Bonnets in the High Street and Vernon Cross' Tea Rooms on Forehill, where the Royal Standard lounge bar is now, served morning coffee and afternoon tea. I once went to a party in Ye Olde Tea Rooms. The shop and café housed Mr Cross' Museum. His collection of swords and helmets decorated the walls and beams.

Fast food of the day was fish and chips, with three of the most popular establishments being where they still are today.

From the 1952 Guide to the City of Ely

From the 1952 Guide to the City of Ely

It Was Fun

There was once a time called childhood. For boys it was a time of Children's Hour and Dick Barton on the radio, Saturday flicks and Cowboys and Indians. It was a time when the goodies beat the baddies. Dinner was at one o'clock, with a roast on a Sunday and tea was sometimes special on that day with tinned peaches and a slice of bread and butter.

It was a time of short trousers, elastic belts with snake buckles, sleeveless pullovers, school caps, balaclava helmets in winter, street cricket and explorations in summer, conkers, coal fires, Turf cigarette cards and comics... all in small type on cheaply printed and produced pages for a few pennies. Available, affordable, readable, followable, swappable, collectable – comics were everything a boy wanted. All there for reading. And, of course, each Christmas there were the comic annuals to look forward to. They were as much a part of Christmas as the turkey and the tree. They provided a wealth of reading during the dark days of winter and they were often kept for many years.

My own love of comics began with the brightly coloured covers of the 'nursery comics' like 'Playbox', 'Rainbow', 'Chicks' Own' and 'Tiny Tots'. From them it was a natural progression to 'Jingles' and one of my regular favourites, 'Tip Top'.

I don't remember learning to read, who does? My grandad's house had very few books, but there were newspapers and magazines and I know that my mother got me some children's books from jumble sales and similar. I only once went, when I was about ten, to the local library which was a couple of wooden huts perched on a site obviously intended for something more permanent. It wasn't an inviting place and none of my family used the library, so neither did I.

Most of my comics came from Burrows newsagents in the High Street and I would lovingly and longingly look at the racks and search the counter for an eye-catching issue. And it was my choice, my small amount of pocket money to be carefully considered. What a disaster, if lured by a colourful cover away from an old and trusted favourite, the contents were disappointing.

Dad's work as an insurance agent took him from door to door 'on his rounds'. One of the great delights for me was sometimes when I accompanied him I would come home with a pile of comics from some householder or he would bring me a pile of comics – 'I wonder if your boy would like these?' Would he!

Sometimes in these wonderful collections of tattered comics would be the publications of Gerald Swan and these fascinated me with eerie tales like 'Krakos the Egyptian' and 'Back from the Dead', the story of Robert Lovett and 'Tulip's Rock Gimlet' stories of an earth-boring machine, all of which could be found in the annuals like the 'Funnies Album'. They were crudely drawn and cheaply produced but real finds. So were the all-colour, (Oh smell the ink!) American 'Superman' and 'Batman' comics that sometimes turned up or came over from one of the nearby American bases along with the comic supplements from the newspapers. My uncles, just back from the army, might have been happy with the rye whiskey and King Edward cigars, which also sometimes came over from the same source, but for me to find a 'Prince Valiant' story made my day!

In 1950 Aunt Rosa gave me a year's subscription to a new comic called 'Eagle' as a present. Soon I was one of a generation of boys following the exploits of Dan Dare, in one of the best remembered and best produced of all children's comics.

Joe Convine, who grew up in the cottage, next to 'Roswell' and left school to work for my grandad and uncle would give me copies of ' Wizard', full of exciting stories, but I did prefer the comics with pictures.

I rang the bells at St Mary's from about 1950 and New Year was magic.

There are eight bells in the tower, and in those days we rang from the ground with about seventy feet of rope. On New Year's Eve the bells were half muffled by strapping a pad to one side of the clapper, so a clear note was produced on one side and on the other a dull note like someone humming.

Bellringing at St Mary's Church, 1952, J.Pickett, M.Thurmott, Ann and M.Grain

From 11.30p.m., the bells would ring out the old year in this fashion for about twenty minutes. Then some brave soul would nip into the bell chamber and remove the muffles.

Old George Vail would step up on to the box necessary to ring the tenor bell which weighs almost a ton. He would spit on his hands, ease the bell off and toll out the dying year, pause a minute of two until twelve o'clock, then strike the hour. On the twelfth note, we would pull off quickly behind him pealing out to welcome the New Year.

After a few minutes, everyone would pause and then crash down all the bells as one, several times. This was called 'firing' and is not done so much these days. It was quite exhilarating at the time.

How we looked forward to the fair when I was young. The carefully hoarded pennies painstakingly spent.

Six pennies (2.5p) squandered on a coloured paper ball stuffed with sawdust on an elastic string to pelt each other. Six pennies to ride on Jollity farm and three to have a go on the hoopla.

Then, very slowly, a penny at a time rolling the last three down a chute on to numbered squares, perhaps winning a few more to extend the evening's enjoyment.

There was a shooting gallery that stood in front of the Corn Exchange. Ping pong balls were sent in to the air on jets of water and young men lined up to knock them off, the spent slugs smacking into the canvas backing. Sometimes they could be found at the foot of the wall after the Fair had gone. That and the colourful, musical Jollity Farm in front of the other side of the Corn Exchange hurtling round up and down are really all I can remember. I never went on the

The family at Hunstanton, Summer 1948: Ruth, Mum, Dad, Ann, with bucket and spade ready, Auntie Edie and Vera (former evacuee)

Jollity Farm, at some early stage in my life I realised that such rides were not for me, I could get dizzy by just watching them.

The same showmen's faces turned up year after year and it was some colour and excitement among the grey days.

I remember my father taking me to the Corn Exchange to watch Boxing events. Sometimes he acted as one of the judges and I sat perched up on the wooden stands relishing the action. The hall would be full, mainly with men and there were several distinguished and well-supported local fighters.

I also saw a table tennis exhibition there. My Uncle Doug was a keen table tennis player and he used to take me to matches at theBeet Factory Social Club with him. In the Corn Exchange, late in 1949, I recall seeing, and getting the autographs of Johnny Leach, the World's Singles Champion, Ken Craigie and Eric Filby, fellow English Internationals, playing against each other and with local players. Again they would draw a big crowd. Apart from the Cinema or going out to the pub, there wasn't much entertainment in Ely at the time.

The Tour De France on television and all its razzamatazz reminded me how important cycling clubs were here at one time. Several contemporaries of mine were committed members of The Littleport Wheelers, and can tell you more tales than I ever could of setting off on Sunday mornings two abreast and sweeping like a snake through the countryside.

Before the war two of my young Bidwell uncles were keen cyclists. Not everyone was competitive, but nearly everyone longed for a racing cycle with drop handles instead of the 'sit up and beg' variety. I cheated and just turned the curved handles on my mum's old bike upside down to give it a sporty look.

There were cycle races at the August Bank Holiday Monday Sports on Paradise. In those days it was at the beginning of August and included all kinds of athletics and displays. A grand day out.

I cannot remember the pre-war events, but I do remember being entertained by the Cossacks. Whether they really came from the Russian Steppes I'll never know. It seems unlikely, as Europe was still in chaos after all the fighting, but they were very exotic. They performed wild tricks on horseback, then on the ground the distinctive dancing with their boots kicking and arms folded. We tried very hard to copy them in the playground afterwards and ended up flat on our behinds.

The other thing that sticks in my mind was the Guinness Clock, a fantastic affair in the mould of Heath Robinson and Roland Emmett. As the clock struck the quarter hour it opened up a series of mechanical movements, most of which escape me at the moment, but I can't remember watching any races that year. We just sat and waited for the clock to leap into action.

I went to the August Bank Holiday Sports, especially as grandad had been on the committee for years, which made it quite easy for me to get in. The Guinness Clock, which was such a big attraction, was one of the touring versions copied from the original one, which had been dreamt up by a Guinness executive for the Festival of Britain in 1951.

In the early 1950's there were also several Shopping Weeks held in the late summer or early autumn. For some of them a large marquee was erected along one side of Paradise and it was filled with trade stands. I enjoyed them. A large tent on grass has a certain smell and feel to it, and I scurried among the various exhibits, being particularly taken with a fighter plane cockpit simulator. We sat in the pilot's seat and grasped the handle, watched the flickering screen ahead of us and shot down as many enemy planers as we could. This was great, and not that many years after the real thing.

The 'Ely Standard' would be reproduced as a fascinating tiny facsimile, so much smaller than the broadsheet weekly that arrived on a Friday.

There were no fireworks when we were small children because of the war. I do vaguely remember indoor fireworks as a rare treat at Christmas. They were rather smelly and the only one I can recall was a tablet, which when ignited rolled out like a snake and then dissolved into ashes.

At the end of the war they fired a lot of green and red flares high into the sky. These were, of course, really intended for the battlefield.

Fireworks when they did appear again were sold in the toy shops at Bolton's and Sykes' and at Burrows, the newsagents. I had, I think, three shillings (15p) to spend. For this I could carefully choose two rockets, a Roman candle, a Catherine wheel, a golden rain and a packet of sparklers. I left the bangers and the jumping crackers to the boys.

They were let off in the back garden, then we scrambled over the fence into the Park, where the King's School boys were allowed to have a bonfire at the bottom of Cherry Hill; definitely not on the cricket pitch which was fenced off. They had more pocket money than us, but most of it went on bangers. It was all a bit dangerous wandering around in the dark, but we survived.

Which is more than I nearly did on one occasion. I was never a great firework fan as a child. I didn't like the bangers but we occasionally had a box of assorted ones to let off down the garden and I remember going round Michael Dyos' for a firework evening.

I would go and watch those school displays in the Park. I didn't take any, but stood high on the slope of Cherry Hill watching the bangs and flashes below.

On this particular evening there was a thump and something landed in the grass near my feet. The boy next to me on my left, bent down and picked the object up and said, 'You save these don't you?'

I glanced round at him briefly, then turned away saying, 'No,' at which point it exploded with an ear splitting bang inches from my left ear. I went deaf, my head rang and I remember stumbling frightened from the dark, gunpowder-smelling Park leaving all the fireworks behind me thinking I had been deafened for life. I didn't even pause to see if the offerer of the gift still had all his fingers. Gradually over the next minutes the whistling in my head lessened, I stopped panicking and my hearing returned.

I felt sad in July 1998 when I read that Tarzan's Jane had passed away. The real Tarzan was Johnny Weissmuller and his Jane was Maureen O'Sullivan. How they delighted us at the pictures on Saturday afternoons at the Public Room Cinema on the Market Place.

The Public Room, later the 'Exchange' Cinema.

Weissmuller had been an Olympic swimmer and his distinctive choppy front crawl, as he swam among the crocodiles, was copied by every would-be champion.

The Tarzan films were already ten years old when we saw them.

The *Public Room*, sited where the Powerhouse Electric showroom is now, seldom had new films. They went to *The Rex*, where Boots is now.

At the *Public Room* we were content for 3d (1.5p) or 6d (2.5p) with Bud Abbot and Lou Costello comedies, Bob Hope and Bing Crosby on the road to somewhere and all the cowboy films. It is the queuing that stands out in my mind. It was a bit of a scrum, you had to stand your ground. Inside it was a scramble for the seats which were well-worn plush, tip-up seats bolted to the flat floor.

There was Roy Rogers, the singing cowboy, and his faithful horse, *Trigger*. Incidentally, did you know he had a dog called Bullet? I didn't until I played Trivial Pursuit one day. There was Hopalong Cassidy, too.

I preferred cowboys and indians to cowboys and crooks. We galloped down the hill home firing imaginary six-shooters.

The newsreels, Pathe Gazette and Gaumont British News, were an important part of going to the cinema. I think they even showed them at the children's matinees and everyone cheered the progress of the war, encouraged by the frightfully posh commentator.

The *Public Room, or Exchange Cinema,* as it became towards the end, was a plain oblong building inside. It had an attractive front, with a clock tower and splendid clock, like many a small town hall. It was demolished along with the Corn Exchange in 1965. What was saved of the clock eventually is now in Ely Museum.

In the mid-fifties, however, the *Public Room* did show a new film, *Rock Around the Clock*. Elsewhere it had cinema-goers stamping and rocking in the aisles. *The Rex* feared for its balcony, so the *Public Room* put it on and stamp we did. Rock 'n' Roll had come to stay.

I didn't go to the 'Public Room' nearly as much as I went to 'The Majestic', but I do remember a gang of us from Silver Street Boy's School going to see Will Hay in 'Oh Mr Porter'. We were about ten, the film was even older, but it was funny and we enjoyed it hugely in that shared experience that the cinema can give.

'The Majestic' was my local cinema as it was at the top of Prickwillow Road in Newnham Street and when I was young I passed it every day on my way to school. I loved the cinema smell of smoke, people and disinfectant that wafted out on to the pavement through its doors. I would look at the posters and study the film stills.

The 'Majestic' was where I went to matinees on Saturday afternoons. There was usually a cliff-hanging serial and cowboy or pirate films. Charles Starratt as the 'Durango Kid' was my great cowboy favourite.

I remember Michael Dyos, who lived almost opposite, winning a painting competition organised by Mr Smith, the Manager.

It wasn't a big cinema. It was advertised as 'The Cosy Cinema' but could seat 370. There was a small foyer with the pay box on the left and once through the doors a sloping auditorium. There were toilets down near the screen on the right hand side. There was no balcony.

One of the last films I saw there, not that many years before it closed in 1959, was 'King Kong', which must have been twenty years old, but I hadn't seen it before and like all the old films shown there, if it was a good rip roaring adventure, we enjoyed it. Most of all though I remember the very smoky and rather hot smelly atmosphere and the usherette walking down the centre aisle spraying a sweet smelling liquid into the air. How the mist of it sparkled in the beam of the projector and how, if I smelt that smell now, I would instantly be back in that warm, dark interior.

The Rex was more luxurious, nine pennies or a shilling for the first six rows. I can't recall how much it cost at *The Majestic*. It had the reputation of being the flea pit and the films shown were coming round for the third time. I did see *Sanders of the River* there. Incidentally, the only flea I ever picked up was at *The Rex*, so we were perhaps doing the *Majestic* a disservice.

The noise at the matinees was deafening. Every now and again the manager would march down and roar at us. Silence descended and we went back to watching Bud Abbot and Lou Costello, Tarzan or Roy Rogers.

What a scramble there was in the intervals for an ice cream from the usherette and her tray. The tubs were rock hard and the choc ices melted and landed in your lap.

I've just remembered how the cigarette smoke drifted up through the beams of light from the projector. The usherettes at *The Rex* paced up and down the aisles with a spray to freshen the air.

Ely has always been fortunate in having a very entertaining amateur dramatic society. The first play I can remember seeing, just after the Second World War, was *Quiet Wedding*.

In those days the Society took over *The Rex*, which had been built as a theatre and a cinema. It had a tiled 1930's façade and entrance smelling vaguely of disinfectant. Inside it was all faded plush and old gold decorations.

It boasted a large auditorium, a balcony and a good-size stage and orchestra pit, which lent itself very well to amateur dramatics and the operatic society.

All this came to an abrupt end in 1954 with Cinemascope and the wide fixed screen being fitted into the *Rex* preventing the use of the stage.

The Society them moved to the Women's Institute Hall, later known as Hereward Hall, which was at the rear of the Rex and from there to the High School Hall and eventually Needham's Hall to continue bringing the pleasure of live theatre to generations of Ely audiences.

My mother loved the amateur dramatics. Her Aunt, Mollie Roythorne had been a stalwart member in past years and Vernon Cross, who was a relative, was one of the mainstays and directed most of the plays.

My mother and my grandma were both members of the Mothers' Union and the Women's Institute. The popular WI met monthly, on a Friday evening, in their hall at the rear of the Rex.

The House that Jack Built' at the WI Hall, 'Jack' is second from the left.

I soon grew to hear with some familiarity the names of some of the eminent members: Mrs Churchyard, Mrs Houghton, Mrs Haylock, Mrs Diver, Mrs Cole... It was through the WI that I was involved in some small plays there. I remember, when I was about nine, 'The House that Jack Built', with my young sister also appearing as the dog. I was Jack and Sally Morriss, whose mother was a keen member and helped with the play, was Mrs Jack. My mother kept the yellowing press account in her papers and according to that also in the play were Jennifer Holmes, Lyn Crick, Janet Beeton, Ann Barton, Jana Drake, David Raine, David Scotting, Kay Wenham, Ann Trevers and Gillian Drake. Mrs Drake was the producer. The play was in mime and the narration was read by a tall, slightly older girl, Sylvia Raine. Tragically a year or two later she collapsed and died at her home. It was the sort of unexplained, sudden death that haunted me when I was young. How could it happen, what if...? Very unsettling when you lived such a protected life as I did.

When I was a few years older, we did a version of ' Snow White and the Seven Dwarfs' with the formidable Mrs Diver. My friend Geoffrey Porter, whose father had a shop in St Mary's Street, opposite the church, played the Prince, I was the Huntsman and Snow White was Christine Taylor, who had a fine singing voice.

The first ADS play my mother took me to was when I was about eleven, It was 'The Chiltern Hundreds' in the Rex. I was hooked. From that moment I was as keen as she was at spotting the distinctive blue print on white playbill posters that announced the new show. Mum had a simple way of telling if the play would be all right: if Geoff Legge, Paddy Bailey, Celia Smith, Allan Franklin and later, Marie Aggas, soon to be Marie Legge, and Ian McKittrick and other regulars were in it, it would be a good show. And they were! Highlights of the year for us.

We also greatly enjoyed the musicals staged by the Operatic Society. I remember 'The Mikado', with Walter Constable, Charles Bush, Peter Barnard, Archie Haylock, Ruby Howes, Olive Beale, Jean Waddington and Vivienne Scott. The last show at the Rex was 'The Lilac Domino', with Paddy Bailey, Geoff Legge and most of the old favourites. It had a delightful title waltz theme that my sister danced to at garden fetes and shows for some years after. Ten years after 'The Chiltern Hundreds', I made my debut with the ADS and my mother came to watch me in 'Sailor Beware', but because of that screen, it was in the WI Hall.

'The Rex', of course, was splendid. Built as a theatre with a stage and orchestra pit, it was far superior to the other two cinemas and had all the latest films. Eventually I graduated to there. I was very into films in my teens and went as often as I could. I saw more films by always going in the cheapest seats. The first six rows cost one shilling (5p). But it was the same film. It was a significant moment when I leapt to the two shilling seats towards the back.

I would go to Burrows and buy 'Picture Show' or 'Picturegoer' and read all about the films and the stars. When I had enough money I would send away for the postcards of my favourites.

Often there were long queues for 'The Rex'. On a Saturday evening, 'Snakey' Blackwell from Burrows would be selling his evening papers in the street outside and the town centre seemed to be full of people. There would be a supporting feature, adverts, the Gaumont British News and, of course, the main feature. A full evening's entertainment for two shillings. Then it was out into the street and the people turning out of the pubs, along to Croot's chip shop, or Lancaster's on the Market Place, for four penn'orth of chips in an open bag. And the long walk home reliving the film and eating the cooling chips. Ah, sadly, the stuff of dreams now.

I never seemed short of things to do when I was young. We started off with Miss Willink and King's Messengers in what was St Mary's Parish Room (now the Kingdom Hall). Around nine years of age, we met to sew small garments for babies in India where Miss Willink had been a missionary and send our pennies out to the children.

Eventually, at about 12, we joined the GFS (Girls' Friendly Society) meeting on Fridays in the Trinity Parish Room. We did a lot of country dancing there and entered competitions in Cambridge. There were three splendid holidays, a real treat in those days. There was Herne

Bay with its high cliffs and Towyn in Wales, where we went hill walking and to the pictures in a tiny cinema with a corrugated roof. *She Wore a Yellow Ribbon* was drowned by a summer storm rattling on the tin. At Shanklin, on the Isle of Wight, I won a prize in the local swimming gala. It was the first time I had competed in the open sea.

We always had a family holiday. Dad had owned a little car of some sort or other since before the War and it was certainly essential for his job. One week in August the car would be packed with boxes and cases. My sister and I would be crammed into the back seat, with this tower of boxes piled up next to us and taller than we were. Wherever we were going it was a major expedition and would take a very long time as the route ran through every village and town on the way. As we turned out of the Drive, the lot would begin to slip and slide over us and we would spend the whole journey shoring it up.

When we had the little caravan we would go to Hunstanton for the vast expanses of sand and the safe paddling, sometimes we went to Great Yarmouth, again in a caravan, a couple of times to Clacton, or more precisely the incredible shanty town of Jaywick. We never went to a holiday camp, mostly caravans, just occasionally a boarding house where rain or shine you had to go out after breakfast and not return until it was time for tea.

I remember two other major expeditions on which my father took me. In August 1948 we spent a day at the Olympic Games at Wembley Stadium. We were nearly level with the track and I remember a French sprinter dropping the baton in a relay. Not much really, but I was there. He also took me to Highbury to watch Arsenal, as I became a fan around the age of ten. It was quite an adventure. We went by car and parked in a side street where some enterprising boys promised to look after our car 'for a tanner'. Which they got, I think dad was afraid that if he didn't pay them, they'd let his tyres down. All I really remember is that the pitch looked to be almost entirely rolled mud, I thought football was played on grass, but this must have been the end of the season and there was precious little grass left. Not much to remember but now I appreciate what a big effort it was to make those trips then.

Michael in his first year at the King's School still in short trousers and sister c.1951

In early teens there was the Youth fellowship on Sunday evenings after Evensong. But best of all there was the Youth Club in Cambridge Road, down the next turning up from the parish hall. It was held in a very suitable building. I have no idea what it was before, but as you went in there was a small office where Mr Russell kept order and two games rooms.

Upstairs a large room with a small rostrum in one corner and I think a kitchen in the other. Four nights a week we amused ourselves there playing table tennis or snooker. Towards the end of the evening a dance or two to records on a wind up gramophone. There was a grand party at Christmas and in Summer camping over at Hemingford Grey with other clubs in the county. We cycled there and back and had the time of our lives. Happy days.

I never went to the Youth Club on Cambridge Road, which in some ways is strange. I think I was too busy with homework or going to the cinema. Why so strange?

My Aunt Rosa lived on Cambridge Road in an old pub, the 'Eagle and Lamb'. I was a frequent visitor there. It was a gloomy, quite large old house and still had all the feeling of being a former public house, with typical public house urinal and toilet in the garden at the rear.

She was widowed not long after she had bought the property in the 1930's. Aunt Rosa, however, did not live alone. Soon after the war had begun, two cousins from London, Uncle Frank Walter and his sister, Florence, Auntie Flo, had arrived with their belongings packed into boxes to stay for the 'duration'.

They were both there long after the war had ended. Auntie Flo, who was in poor health, hardly leaving the dark sweet smelling front room where she lived and I was sent in to kiss her soft pale cheek. Uncle Frank pottering round isolated by his deafness offering me liquorice toffees. Aunt Rosa, a fiercely independent woman, cared for them both.

Her property included a yard to the rear. At the bottom of the yard was a former meat pie factory, which had been converted into the Youth Club. Aunt Rosa was the landlord and my father helped her with her business affairs. He had many dealings with the Youth Club, but I was never a member.

We once tripped the light fantastic where now you park your car at Tesco. It was the Railway Social Club at Ted Day's old time dances.

About 1951 I first went to classes run by Ted Day with a wind up gramophone and 78s. The clubhouse was an old ex-army round-topped Nissen hut made from corrugated iron, but we Tipsy Two-Stepped and Empress Tango'd with the best of them. There was the Barn Dance and the Palais Glide, the Dashing White Sergeant and the Gay Gordons. Titter ye not, we had the time of our lives.

We also danced to his band, the Melody Aces. I can remember Mrs Futter on the piano and Alfie Sergeant on the drums, but there were many other musicians over the years.

No teenage ravers today enjoy themselves better than we did. Brylcream glistened, pin curls were perfected, the air was perfumed with White Fire, L'Aiment and Phulnana. Circular skirts and stiletto heels, sports jackets and flannels, suits on Saturdays; all quite formal and tremendous fun.

One winter evening the red liquid polish on the concrete floor melted from the friction of dancing feet and condensation. It stuck to the soles of precious dancing shoes and soaked into trouser turnups.

Ann with Swimming Club Trophies
1952/3

Sometimes the dances were held in the Central Hall in Market Street, where the parquet floor was like glass by comparison.

At some point, about 1954, the venue changed to the Drill Hall in Barton Road. I often waved a partner off on the midnight bus to Soham from Barton Square, then trotted home to Broad Street in the pitch dark quite happily.

I can only recall going to a few dances when they moved to the Corn Exchange. The modern dance with its quicksteps, foxtrots and jitterbugs had always been held there, but I wasn't considered old enough to go there in its heyday.

And then came rock 'n' roll. Not to be beaten Mr Day devised an old time rock 'n' roll.

A lasting memory of this energetic dance was losing hold of a partner's sweating hand and sliding across the floor into folding chairs. How embarrassing.

At some time, I understand, old time dances moved to Hereward Hall in Newnham Street, but by then I was over the hills and far away.

Sometime in my early teens I became a regular attender of the charity ball for young people in aid of Dr Barnardo's Homes. It was held in the Drill Hall on Barton Road early in the year.

To prepare us for the event so we didn't trample the feet of the poor girls too badly, some dancing classes were held. The teacher was Mrs McKittrick and a very good lively teacher she was too. At one time the classes were held in the barn-like room next to St Mary's Vicarage. There we were put through our paces while the gramophone poured out a Joe Loss or Victor Sylvester strict tempo waltz or quick step.

Then carrying our patent leather dance shoes in a brown paper bag, or tucked into our coat pockets, we would eventually arrive, dressed in our father's evening suits with black bow tie, to the event. My father would drive my partner and me there and collect us afterwards. It was at that time one of the social highlights of our year. One of them? For a while, probably the only social highlight of our young years.

But what did I need with a social life? School with its homework, plenty of sport and acting seemed to occupy me fully. New friendships were almost all based on school with Ross, Adam, Chris and John and his sister Jennifer from just along Lynn Road and her friend, Janet from Orchard Estate. There was the cinema and cycling everywhere I could. Ely was my world and it suited me.

Dad became an Urban District Councillor and lived and breathed it and we found our lives increasingly centred on that. I still got round to 'Roswell' as often as I could. Uncle Doug had married Auntie Polly. Uncle Cliff and Auntie Pip had built a new bungalow in Lynton Close on the fields on which we used to play. Things were changing, of course. Ely had electric street lights for one thing. Elvis Presley was having an influence from across the Atlantic and sideboards were not just something we all had in our living rooms.

I didn't know what I wanted to do when I left school. That was a long way ahead, but my precious, protected, childhood was slipping into the past and I don't think I had any real idea what a good and fortunate one it had been.

Afterwords

On the day I left school at 16 I took the Railway Exam and medical. The following week I started work in the Goods Office at Ely for £1.50 a week. This crept up to nearly £4.00 by the time I left in 1957.

From then on it was here, there and everywhere at the whim of the Fleet Air Arm or the Buckinghamshire Constabulary. A short spell on a farm way out in Swaffham Prior Fen, somewhere in the middle. All tied houses with their inherent problems. I got so I could pack up and move in a day.

Back to Ely in 1969 and the Civil Service for fourteen years. This was when I was thankful I had been unwittingly channelled from school into clerical work rather than shorthand typing. Pen pushing, it was equal pay for equal work. Like the railway I was paid the same as male colleagues and I could keep a roof over our head.

In August 2001 I retired after fifteen years six months in the Cathedral. Magnificent surroundings but I was happy not to have to tackle another winter. By the time I put on all my winter togs I felt like a Michelin Man. Several hours sitting in the cold makes you feel quite mouldy,

I can count myself lucky we were never out of work, like the generation before and the one after. The dole queue did not haunt my working life.

I enjoyed my sport and acting at the King's School, but I left the school with little thought of university and went into the drawing office of the Ely Urban District Council. Mr Shilston was the Engineer and Surveyor and Mr Watkins was the Clerk of the Council. The offices were in the former fire station, next to the police station and court house on Lynn Road. We could not open the windows of the drawing office because those who lived in the old gaol house had a right to privacy in their garden. Two years later, by which time Geoffrey Stroud had become the Engineer, I left for Kesteven College of Education to train as a teacher.

I enjoyed three good years at Stoke Rochford, near Grantham, then taught at a primary school in north London, a secondary school and a primary school in March, before really returning to familiar territory and taking up a one term appointment at Soham Village College under Peter Riggulsford, the then Warden. That term has extended to the present day.

Along the way I continued to enjoy my sport, playing cricket, rugby and tennis for Ely and also amateur dramatics with Ely ADS, College Players, Soham, and later appearing with and directing for the Campaign Amateur Theatre in Ely.

In 1970 I followed my father into local government, serving as Mayor of Ely from 1976-77 and Chairman of East Cambridgeshire District Council from 1986-88. I am still proud to serve on the City of Ely parish council. During those years I was a founder member of the Ely Society and the Ely Museum.

It was the late Reg Holmes who really sparked an enthusiasm in me in Ely's history, and writing developed as an interest with several books on Ely, two on Soham, Cambridge, Cambridgeshire and the East Anglian Coast.

Grandad Unwin died in 1957, my grandmother in 1973, my dear mother died in 1981 and my father in 1985. I left Lynton Drive and all its memories. By then nearly every area I had played on as a child was built on. Now the 'Rifleman's Arms' just round the corner, renamed in recent years by its original name 'The Tinker of Ely', has been demolished and replaced by town houses, just like the old 'Rising Sun' went many years ago, along with my grandfather's old workshop and orchard as a housing development.

Uncle Doug died in 1999, but Auntie Polly still lives in 'Roswell', the house that contains so many of my childhood memories.

My Sister, after marrying Brunello Nardone, an Italian business man and living in Naples, returned to live in Ely some years ago and her son, Raoul, having gained a good degree in Fine Arts is working for a design company in London.

I am sad that my parents never saw my own family. I married Maxine in 1990 and we have Ben, who is now nine, Lauren, who is seven, Lee who is five and Cassie who is three. And what of their childhood? Central heating ('What was coal, Daddy?'), colour television, and 'The Tweenies', 'Fireman Sam' and videos, Power Rangers and transformer toys, computers and computer games, only occasional trips to the cinema, but 'Burger King' and Chinese take-aways, supermarket shopping and travelling by people carrier. There's pop music and disco dancing, fashion clothes and trainers (what was wrong with plimsolls?) but sadly little freedom to roam and explore on their own. I hope though it is a happy childhood.

For me - life is full and rewarding (and tiring!) and one in which, rarely does a day go by, that I don't think, with gratitude, of those who gave me the childhood I enjoyed.

From the 1952 Guide to the City of Ely

From the 1952 Guide to the City of Ely